MARBLES

101 Ways to Play

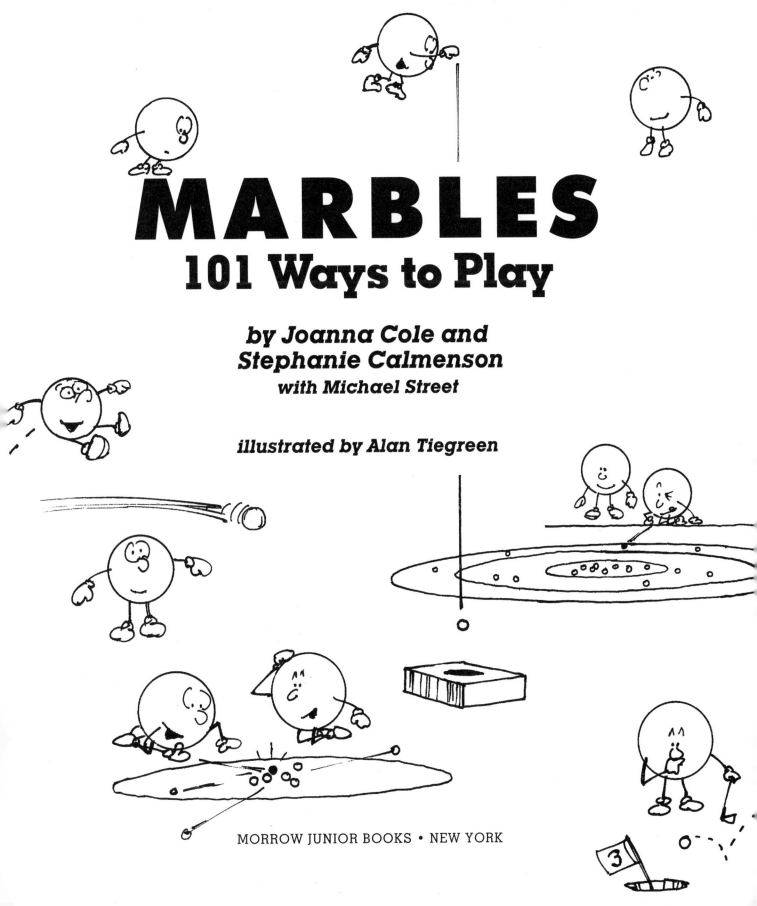

MARBLES
101 Ways to Play

by Joanna Cole and
Stephanie Calmenson
with Michael Street

illustrated by Alan Tiegreen

MORROW JUNIOR BOOKS • NEW YORK

Special thanks to Jim Ridpath, Dennis Webb,
and especially Bertram Cohen (also known as "Mr. Marbles")
for sharing their extensive knowledge of the history of marbles and marble games.

Published by Morrow Junior Books
a division of William Morrow and Company, Inc.
1350 Avenue of the Americas, New York, NY 10019
www.williammorrow.com

Printed in the United States of America.

1   2   3   4   5   6   7   8   9   10

Library of Congress Cataloging-in-Publication Data
Cole, Joanna.
Marbles/Joanna Cole and Stephanie Calmenson with Michael Street; illustrated by Alan Tiegreen.
p. cm.
Summary: Traces the history of marbles and marble making, gives instructions for playing various kinds of games,
explains related terms, and suggests further activities.
ISBN 0-688-12205-1
1. Marbles (Game)—Juvenile literature.   [1. Marbles (Game).   2. Games.]   I. Calmenson, Stephanie.
II. Street, Michael.   III. Tiegreen, Alan, ill.   IV. Title.   GV1213.C65 1998   796.2—dc21   97-36251   CIP AC

CONTENTS

MARBLES
101 Ways to Play

THE HISTORY OF MARBLES

The game of marbles has been around for thousands and thousands of years. If you visit the British Museum in London, you can see clay, stone, and flint marbles that date back to the ancient Romans and Egyptians. But it wasn't until the 1800s that marbles, as we know them today, were born.

The name *marble* actually comes from the kind of stone that was once used to make marbles. During the 1800s, the best playing pieces were made from a type of white marble called alabaster. But because alabaster was very expensive, people began making marbles out of clay. Although clay marbles were less expensive to make, they chipped or broke easily. So marble makers began to experiment with other kinds of materials, such as china and glass, but those marbles were also too costly to make. Finally, in 1846, a German glassblower invented special scissors that could make marbles, and marbles became cheap and easy to produce. This revolutionary tool simply snipped off a little glob of melted glass, which was then shaped to form a marble.

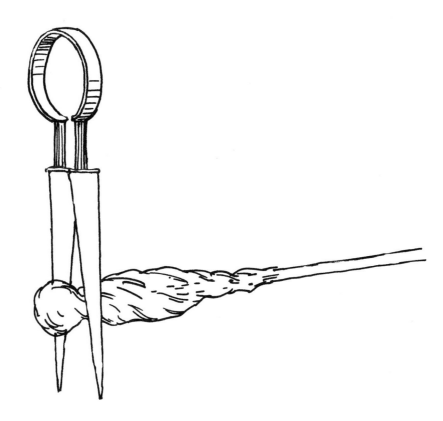

Today glass marble making is done in factories, where hot glass is dropped onto steel rollers that shape it into marbles. Marble making has always been environmentally friendly, because recycled glass makes the strongest marbles. Scrap glass from bottles, jars, and other sources is put into a white-hot furnace for several hours before it is ready to be made into marbles.

Marbles can also be made by hand. There are over one hundred glassmakers in the United States who make one-of-a-kind marbles, each with its own design. These handmade marbles have become popular collector's items.

You can find marbles in lots of places, including flea markets, antiques shops, garage sales, marble auctions, and marble shows. Today nearly five billion machine-made marbles are produced every year.

BEFORE YOU BEGIN

MARBLE BASICS
What is this game, anyway?

Because marbles have been around for so many years, there are hundreds of different games to play. But you'll find that certain rules and terms are always the same, so we'll explain those first.

Almost all marble games involve shooting a marble—usually one that is larger than the others—at one or more target marbles lying on the ground. The shooting marble is called a *shooter*, *taw*, or *boss*. The target marble is called a *mib* or *kimmie*.

Some games have a *taw line* that you must stand behind while you are shooting. Players take turns shooting at the mibs until all of the marbles are gone from the ground, or until one player has won all or most of the marbles. Extra turns can sometimes be won with successful shots, and players sometimes have to pay a penalty of one or more marbles for a bad shot.

MARBLE STAKES
Friendlies or keepsies?

One of the most important decisions to make before you start a game of marbles is whether you'll be playing *friendlies* or *keepsies*.

The difference is very simple. When you play friendlies, all the players get their marbles back at the end of the game, regardless of who won or lost. If you play keepsies, you keep every marble that you win. This is a good way to lose your marbles when you're not yet good at the game. We recommend that you play friendlies most of the time, especially when you're first learning.

If you're playing friendlies, be sure to keep track of how many marbles each player has put into the game, especially when players must pay penalties, which means to give up marbles to another player. It's easiest to keep track when each player uses a different kind of marble.

MARBLE SURFACES
Where can we play these games?

One of the great things about marbles is that you can play inside or outside, on almost any flat surface you can find. There are some places that make it hard to shoot a marble straight, though. Any room indoors with smooth wood or linoleum floors is good, but thick carpets or wrinkly rugs can slow down your shooter or push it off-course.

If you want to take your game outside, look for a flat artificial surface that isn't sloped and is out of the way of other people. Good places to play are sidewalks, asphalt playgrounds, and tennis courts. You can also play on dirt, though marbles may fall in a hole or get stuck in a rut. Serious marble players avoid playing on dirt for these reasons.

Don't play marbles in or near the street, and stay away from deep holes, such as drains or sewer gratings, where you could lose a marble.

If you need to mark up a surface (if you're drawing a circle for the circle games, for example), chalk works best outdoors because it's bright and washes off easily from most surfaces. When you're playing indoors or someplace where chalk doesn't work, use masking tape or lay down a string or thread. Be sure to use thin string so it doesn't stop marbles from rolling out of the ring.

PLAYING MARBLES

HOW TO SHOOT A MARBLE
Here's how the pros do it

Now that you've picked a good place to play, it's time to learn how to shoot a marble. Players usually pick a larger marble to be their shooter, or shooting marble. If you want to play officially, according to tournament rules, your shooter should be no bigger than 3/4", but any larger marble will generally do. You and your friends can decide if you want to play with steelies, which can often damage the target marbles.

There are several ways to shoot your marbles, and certain games will require you to shoot different ways. The easiest way is called *fulking*.

• Hold your shooter with the second knuckle of your forefinger, as shown. Your hand does not need to touch the ground.

• Brace your thumb behind the marble and then flick your thumb forward, pushing your marble forward.

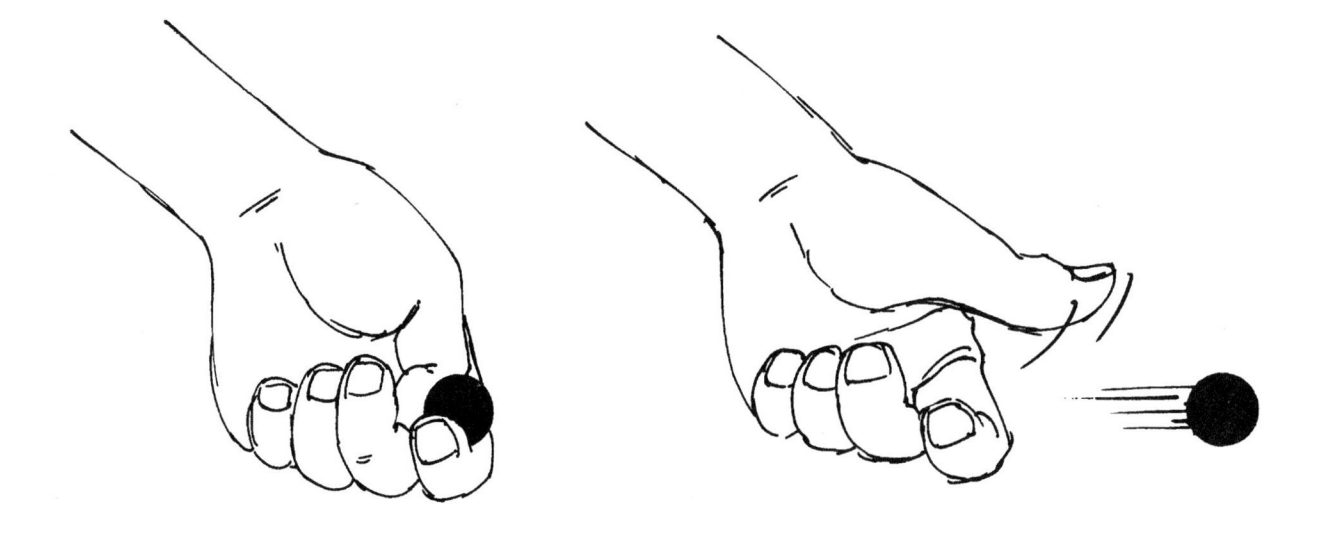

In India, players shoot their marbles by catapulting them forward with their middle finger, as shown. The first and ring fingers must be held on the ground.

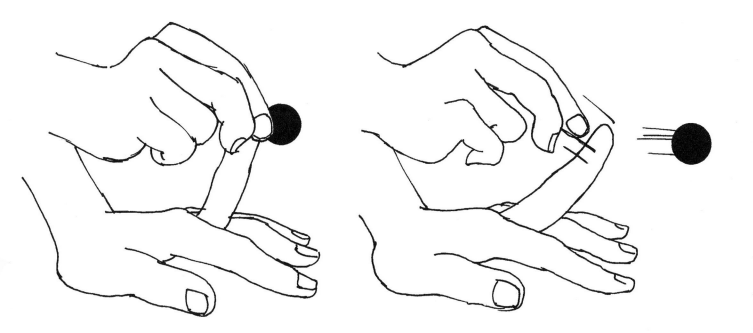

Another way to shoot is to *knuckle down*, which is the method most tournaments (and almost all of the games in this book) will require you to use. As a beginner, you'll probably find it easier not to knuckle down, but it's a skill you'll need to learn if you want to play serious marbles.

At least one knuckle (and sometimes all four) must remain on the ground while you are shooting. Lifting up your hand or moving it forward is called *fudging*, *histing*, *hunching*, or *scrumpy knuckling*.

- Crouch or kneel down, and lay your hand, palm up, comfortably in front of you, so that you won't want to move it when you shoot.

- Place your shooter so that it rests in the space between your first and second fingers.

- Curl your forefinger around the shooter and curl the rest of your fingers behind it.

- Put your thumb behind your shooter, bracing it with your middle finger.

- Flick your thumb forward, shooting the marble out.

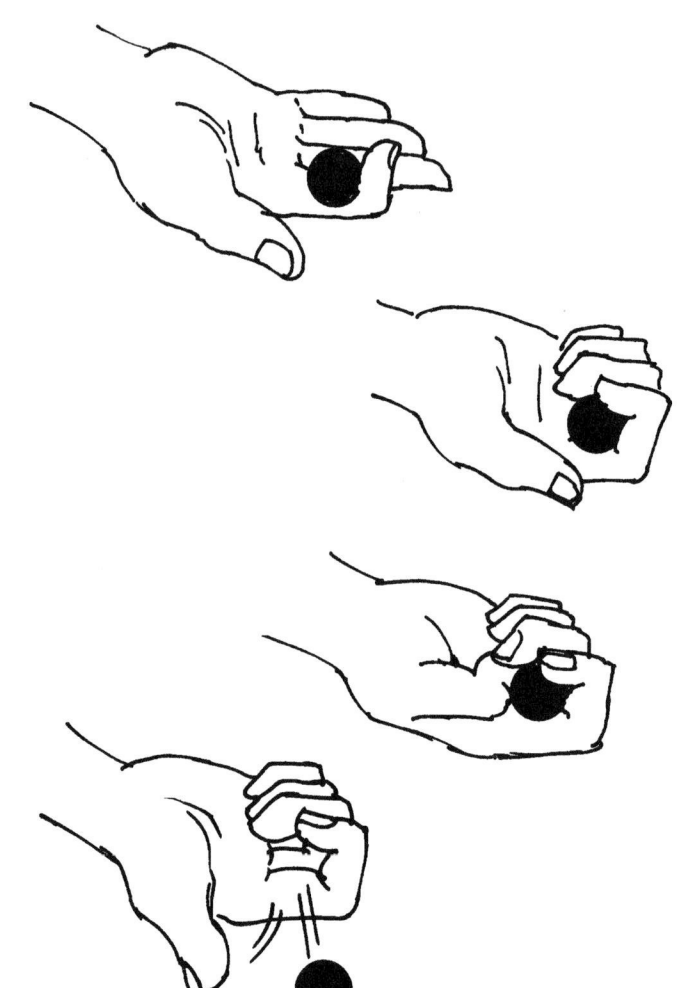

No matter which way you shoot, you will want to line up your shot, which means crouching down low enough so you can see from your shooter to the marble you're aiming at.

Most of the time, your shooter will hit the ground, then roll all the way to the mib, or target marble. Sometimes, though, you will want to shoot your marble through the air in an arc in order to hit the marble (*lofting*). Or try *plunking*—shooting your marble so that it hits the target without hitting the ground first. Practice all these shots to be an expert marble player, or *mibster*.

When you are comfortable with knuckling down, you can try to put backspin on your shooter. Backspin will make your shooter stay in place after it hits the mib, which is useful in Ring Taw and many other games, when it's important to keep your shooter in the ring.

To put backspin on your marble, hold it as if you were going to knuckle down. But as you shoot, keep pressure on the marble with your forefinger, tipping your hand forward if the game allows you to. It may feel like the marble is squirting out of your fingers, but when you do it correctly, the shooter will strike, then spin in place so that it doesn't roll too far.

Some games require you to drop the marble from above, rather than shoot it. This is called *bombsies*, and it's the easiest way to shoot. Stand up and extend the hand with your shooter in it until your arm is straight in front of you. Hold the marble at the same level as your eye. Drop it. That's all there is to it!

LAGGING

The classic way to decide who's going to shoot first

To decide which player goes first, draw two lines, the *lag line* and the *shooter's line*, on the ground. You can agree on a different distance, but in tournaments, these two lines are ten feet apart.

Everyone stands behind the shooter's line and tries to get his or her marble closest to the lag line. Players can knuckle down, toss their marbles, or roll them like bowling balls—it's their choice. When everyone has taken his or her turn, the player with the marble closest to the line goes first.

WHAT'S IN A SPAN?
A common marble measurement explained

Span is a word you'll use a lot when you play marbles. It can mean two different things: either a measurement or a type of shot.

When it is used as a measurement, a span is the farthest distance between the extended thumb and any finger (usually the middle one), as shown. To prevent disagreements, in some games a span is measured by the largest (or smallest) hand in the game.

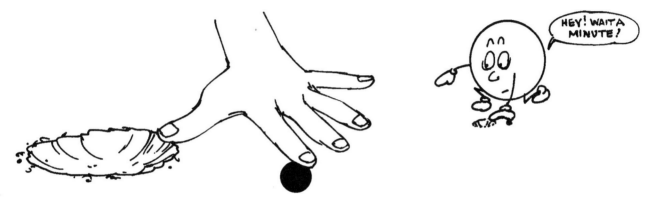

In a span shot, the shooter and mib must be within a span of each other. To span two marbles, place your thumb outside one marble and another finger of the same hand outside the other marble. (Some games may require players to use a particular finger.) With one motion, bring your finger and thumb together, trying to knock the marbles against each other. A successful span shot usually means the player keeps the mib and takes another turn.

EASY TO CHALLENGING MARBLES
Changing the game so it's right for you

We've rated each of the games in this book on a scale from one to three marbles, a one-marble game being the kind that practically anyone can pick up quickly and start playing. This rating is based partly on how difficult the rules are to understand and partly on how hard a particular game is to win. But don't worry if a three-marble game sounds too challenging or a one-marble game too easy. There are plenty of ways to change the rules to make a game easier or more challenging. These ideas will also help you invent new games or customize old ones by figuring out what kinds of rules you and your friends like best. Rules vary in different neighborhoods and parts of the country because kids change them. The only hard and fast rule in marbles is for everyone to have fun!

EASY   NOT AS EASY   HARD

One way to change a game is to move the taw line farther away or closer to you. You can also remove it entirely. If your game has a circle or a square in it, you can make it bigger or smaller. Or you can change the shooting rules—make players knuckle down, let them shoot bombsies, or require all shots to be made by plunking. In hole games, you'll quickly discover that marbles roll easily into holes with steep sides, while you may have trouble getting a mib into a shallow-sided hole. If some players are better shooters than others, you can make them knuckle down, shoot with smaller marbles, or stand farther away. And the best way to make a marble game easy is to play friendlies, so nobody goes away feeling bad.

TERMS YOU NEED TO KNOW

Bombsies   Shooting at a marble from above. Stand next to the marble (or behind the taw line, depending on the game) and hold your shooter just below your eye. Line up your shot by looking past your shooter at the target marble and let the shooter go.

Boss   Another word for *shooter*.

Dropsies   Another term for *bombsies*.

Friendlies   Playing marbles so that all the marbles get returned to their original owners at the end of the game, regardless of whether other players have "won" those marbles or not. The opposite of *keepsies*.

Fudging   Moving your shooting hand forward while shooting. Also called *hunching*.

Fulking   A method of shooting a marble without knuckling down.

Histing   Lifting your knuckles while shooting.

Hunching   Moving your shooting hand forward while shooting. Also called *fudging*.

Keepsies   Playing marbles so that players keep all the marbles won during a game. The opposite of *friendlies*.

Kimmie   Another word for *mib*, or target marble.

Knuckle down   A strict shooting style (also called *knucks* or *knuckles*) used in all tournaments and most serious marble games, in which the shooter must keep one or more knuckles on the ground at all times during the shot.

Lagging   An easy way to figure out who shoots first. Players draw two lines, then stand behind one and toss marbles at the other. The player whose marble lands closest to the second line shoots first.

Lofting   A method of shooting that makes the shooter fly through the air rather than roll on the ground.

Mib   The target marble(s) you are trying to hit.

Mibster   A marble player.

Plunking   Shooting the marble so that it hits the target marble without hitting the ground first.

Scrumpy-knuckling   Another term that means *histing*.

Shooter   Either the player taking the shot, or the marble the player shoots with. Shooter marbles are sometimes (but not always) larger than regular marbles and are usually prized by their owners.

Span   The farthest distance between the extended thumb and any finger, used as a measurement in marbles. It also means holding two marbles at a span length, with the thumb behind one and another finger behind the other, and then trying to push the marbles together.

Straight-arm bombsies   Like bombsies, but a player must hold the shooter at arm's length (and therefore can't line up his or her shot).

Taw   Another word for *shooter*.

Taw line   The line you stand behind to shoot at target marbles. Most games have a taw line.

CIRCLE GAMES

These will keep you going around and around

Every June for the past seventy-five years, kids from across America have gathered at the National Marbles Tournament in Wildwood, New Jersey, to find out who's the mightiest mibster in the country. Ringer, the first game in this section, is what they play at this tournament. It's one of the most popular circle games around.

Once you've mastered that game, you'll want to try some other traditional circle games, like Ring Taw or Increase Pound. Take aim from above in Bounce Eye and Dropsies, or let your ring become a square or a triangle for games like Knuckle Box and Skelly.

RINGER
Play the official version first

Number of mibsters: Two or more (best with two)
Difficulty: 🔮 🔮
Object of game: To hit the marbles out of the ring

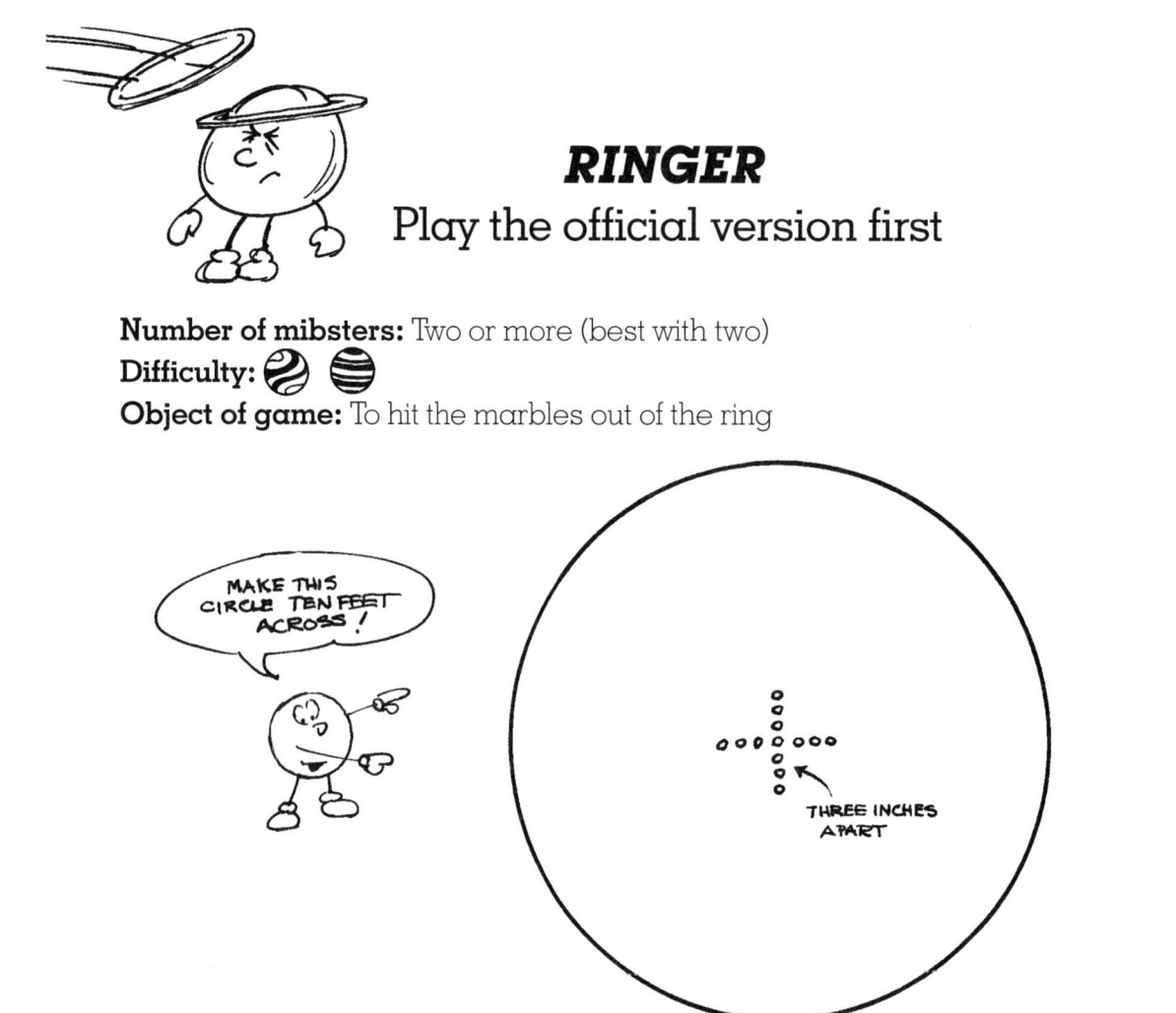

1. Draw a circle that is ten feet across and put thirteen marbles in it. The marbles should be in a cross, as shown, and spaced three inches apart.

2. Starting with the first player, each mibster shoots from anywhere outside the circle, trying to hit a mib out of the ring while keeping her shooter inside the ring. Tournament rules say that players must knuckle down when they shoot.

3. If a player's shooter misses a mib, or doesn't hit any out of the ring, her turn is over and she picks up her shooter.

4. If her shooter hits a mib out of the ring but the shooter also rolls out of the ring, she keeps the marbles that rolled out of the ring. Her turn is over, however, and she picks up her shooter.

5. If her shooter hits a mib out of the ring and stays inside the ring, then she gets to shoot again. She keeps all the marbles that she hit out of the ring, but she has to shoot from wherever her shooter ends up.

6. On each new turn, players can shoot from anywhere outside the circle. Play continues until all the marbles have been shot out of the ring.

7. Whoever ends up with the most marbles is the winner.

Variation:

If a player misses her shot and her shooter remains inside the circle, she must leave her shooter where it lies. That marble then becomes a target for other players, who can keep it if they knock it out of the ring.

RING TAW
The classic form of Ringer

Number of mibsters: Two or more
Difficulty:
Object of game: To knock marbles out of the inner circle

1. Draw a circle on the ground, about seven feet across. Inside that circle, draw a smaller one that is one foot across.

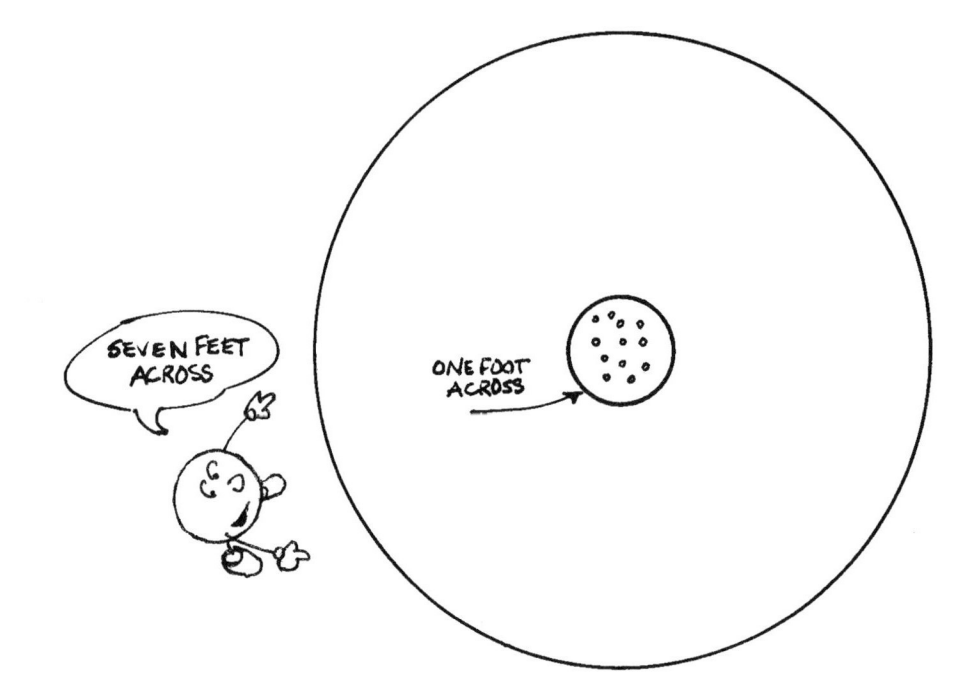

2. Each player contributes the same number of mibs (one to five is a good range) and puts them in the inner circle.

3. Starting with the first player, each player shoots from anyplace outside the outer circle on the first turn. On every turn after his first, however, a player must shoot from wherever his shooter is.

4. If a player knocks a mib outside the inner circle, he keeps that marble and continues to shoot. He must shoot from wherever his shooter ends up.

5. If a player doesn't hit any marbles out of the circle, his turn is over.

6. Players can also shoot at other players' shooters inside either circle. If one is hit (it doesn't need to be knocked out of either ring), the owner must pay the player who hit it one marble. A player can't hit the same shooter twice in the same turn.

7. The game ends when there are no mibs left in either circle. The player who gets the most marbles is the winner.

Variation:
In order to keep a mib (and continue his turn), a player must shoot the mib out of the large circle.

ENGLISH RING TAW
A very proper variation of Ring Taw

Number of mibsters: Two or more

Difficulty: 🔴 🔵

Object of game: To hit the mibs out of the ring and keep your shooter outside the ring

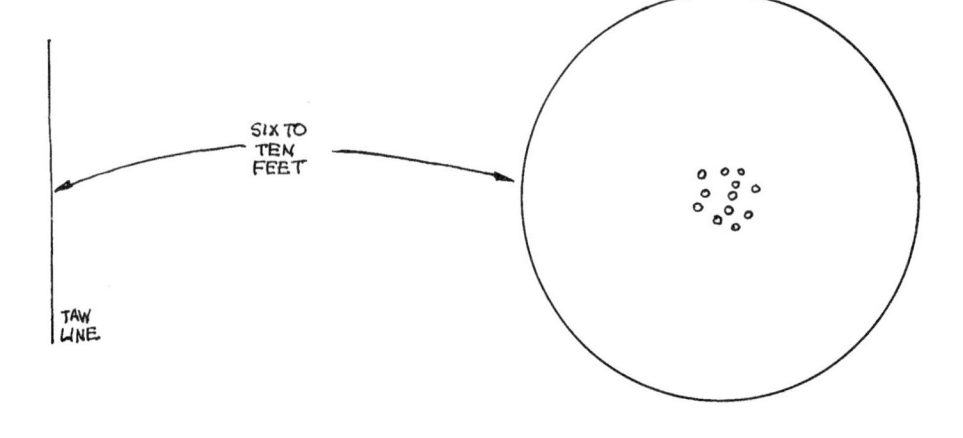

SIX TO TEN FEET

TAW LINE

1. Draw a circle a few feet across (the smaller the circle, the easier the game). Mark a taw line six to ten feet away from the edge of the circle, depending on how well you can shoot. Each player contributes the same number of mibs (one to five is a good range) and puts them in the circle.

2. The first player begins the game by shooting from behind the taw line. She needs to hit the mibs out of the ring and keep her shooter outside the ring too. Players can keep any marbles that they hit out of the circle, but any shooters remaining in the ring become targets for other players.

3. If a player hits a mib out of the circle but her shooter stays in the circle, she can continue her turn by shooting with any

marble she has already won. Her shooter then remains in the ring and becomes a target for other players.

4. If a player hits a mib outside the circle and her shooter also ends up outside the circle, she continues her turn by shooting from anywhere behind the taw line.

5. If a player doesn't hit anything, her turn is over, and the next player gets to shoot. If the shooter stays in the circle, she has to leave it there. If her shooter ends up outside the circle, she can keep it and begin her next turn by shooting from anywhere behind the taw line.

6. If a player has no more marbles to shoot with, she's out of the game.

7. The game ends when all the marbles have been knocked out of the circle. The player with the most marbles wins.

INCREASE POUND

A game to make your marble bag heavier

Number of mibsters: Two or more
Difficulty: 🌀 🌍 🌑
Object of game: To hit mibs out of the pound

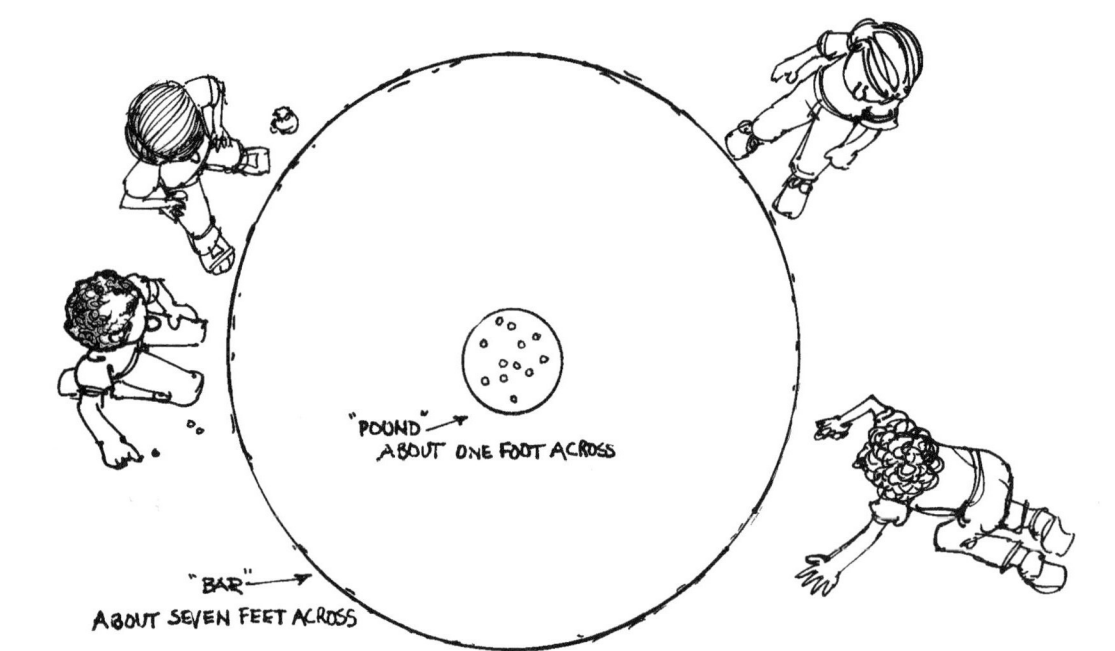

"POUND"
ABOUT ONE FOOT ACROSS

"BAR"
ABOUT SEVEN FEET ACROSS

1. Draw a circle on the ground, about seven feet across. Inside that circle, draw a smaller one, about one foot across. The inner circle is called the *pound* and the outer ring is called the *bar*. Each player should put the same number of marbles into the pound.

2. Players take turns shooting from outside the bar, trying to hit mibs out of the pound. Any mib hit out of the pound is kept by the player who hits it, but that player does not continue his turn.

3. When a player's shooter ends up inside the pound, he must pay one marble into the pound before removing the shooter. If the shooter ends up outside the pound but inside the bar, it must remain there and become a target for other players. Shooters ending up outside both circles can be shot from anywhere outside the bar on the next turn. These rules apply whether or not the shooter has hit any mibs.

4. If a player hits another player's shooter, the player who owns that shooter must put one marble into the pound and give all the marbles he has won in the game to the player who hit his shooter.

5. The game is over when no more marbles remain inside the ring.

Variation:

For a simpler game, have the player whose shooter is hit pay one marble to the player hitting his shooter. He is not required to forfeit all of the marbles he has won.

FORTIFICATIONS

Shoot your way to the fort in the center

Number of mibsters: Two or more
Difficulty: 🌀 🌐 🌀
Object of game: To shoot all the mibs out of all four circles

EIGHT FEET ACROSS
SIX FEET ACROSS
FOUR FEET ACROSS
TWO FEET ACROSS

1. Draw four circles on the ground, one inside the other, as shown. The largest circle should be about eight feet across, and each smaller circle should be about two feet narrower than the last.

2. Each player puts three marbles in the center circle (also called the *fort*), two marbles in the next circle, and one marble in the third circle. The outer ring remains empty.

3. The first player shoots her shooter from anywhere outside the largest circle, aiming only at the marbles in the third ring. If she hits a marble in any other ring out of its circle, she must return it to its original spot.

4. If she hits a mib out of the third circle, she keeps the mib and her turn is over.

5. If she doesn't hit any mibs, she must pay one marble into the fort, and her turn is over. This penalty will continue throughout the game, no matter which ring a player is aiming at.

6. In any case, she leaves her shooter wherever it lands. If it is outside the outer ring, she may shoot on her next turn from anywhere outside the circle. Players may shoot at other players'

shooters, but they don't keep them if they hit them. If asked, a player must lift her shooter to allow another player a clear shot at a mib. She must replace her shooter in the same place after the shot, however.

7. Players continue until all marbles have been shot out of the third ring. Play then continues with the next player aiming at the marbles in the second ring.

8. If a player hits a mib in the second ring, she is entitled to one extra shot. Even if her second shot hits another marble, her turn is over after the second shot.

9. When all the mibs have been cleared from the second ring, players begin shooting at the marbles in the fort.

10. Hitting a mib in the fort can give a player up to two extra turns, as long as she hits another marble out on her second turn.

11. When all the marbles are gone from the center circle, the game is over. The player with the most marbles wins.

POTSIES
Win all the marbles, or win nothing at all

Number of mibsters: Two or more
Difficulty: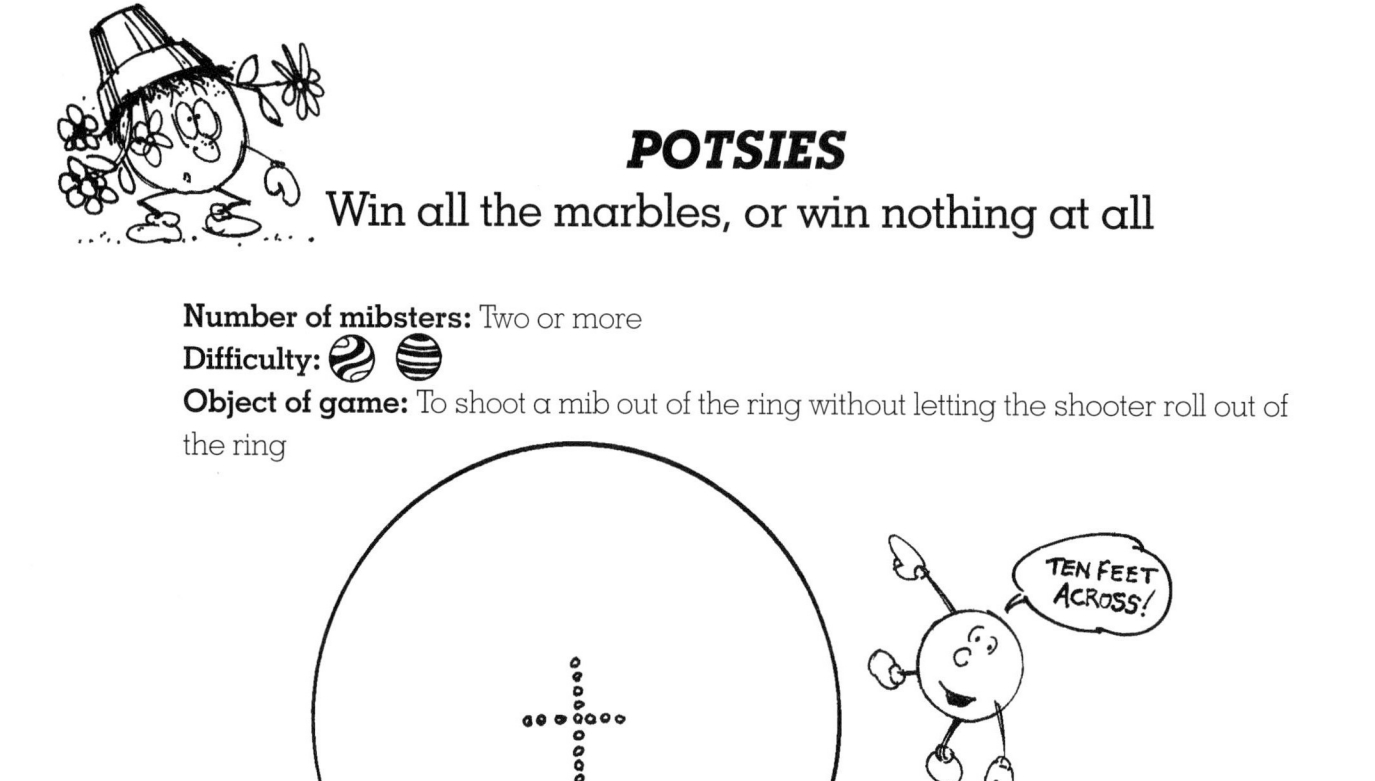
Object of game: To shoot a mib out of the ring without letting the shooter roll out of the ring

TEN FEET ACROSS!

1. Draw a circle that is ten feet across. Each player puts the same number of marbles in the ring, and the marbles are arranged in a cross in the middle of the circle.

2. Players must shoot by knuckling down. They take turns shooting outside of the ring, trying to shoot a mib out of the ring without letting the shooter roll out of the ring too. If a player fails to hit any mibs out, his turn is over.

3. If a player shoots a mib out but his shooter rolls out too, he does not keep the mib. He replaces the mib in the ring (as close as possible to the spot it was in before) and picks up his shooter. His turn is over.

4. If a player shoots a mib out and his shooter stays in the ring, he may shoot again from where his shooter ended up.

5. The game ends when one player wins more marbles than he contributed. He is the winner. If you're playing keepsies, he collects all the marbles originally in the circle (even those won by other players).

BOUNCE EYE

Aim carefully and let your shooter fly!

Number of mibsters: Two or more
Difficulty:
Object of game: To knock mibs out of the circle by shooting bombsies

1. Draw a circle on the ground; the circle can be anywhere from one foot to five feet across, depending on how good your bombing skills are.

2. Each player puts the same number of marbles (one to three) into the ring. They can be piled up or scattered around the ring.

3. Players take turns standing outside the circle and shooting bombsies, trying to knock mibs out of the circle.

4. If any mibs leave the circle, the player who knocked them out collects the mibs and her shooter, and her turn is over.

5. If no mibs leave the circle, the player must pay one marble into the middle and collect her shooter. Her turn is over.

6. The game is over when all the mibs have been knocked out of the circle. The player with the most marbles wins.

Variations:

1. If a player does not hit any mibs and her shooter stops inside the circle, she must leave her shooter in the ring. Other players may then aim at her shooter.

2. Another variation is called Stand Up Megs. The only difference in the rules is that players have to stand two feet away from the edge of the circle and toss their marbles into the circle. No bombsies allowed.

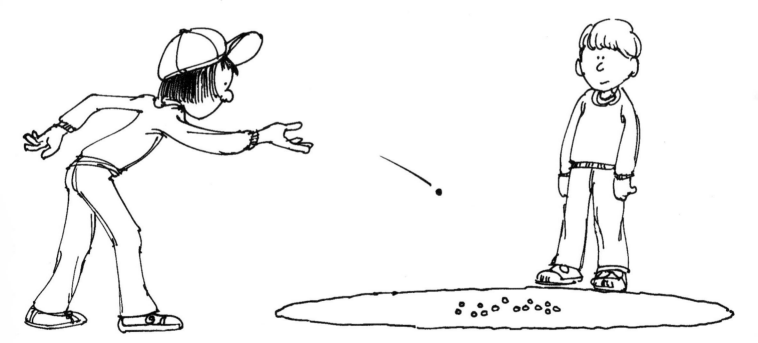

DROPSIES
Watch out below!

Number of mibsters: Two or more
Difficulty: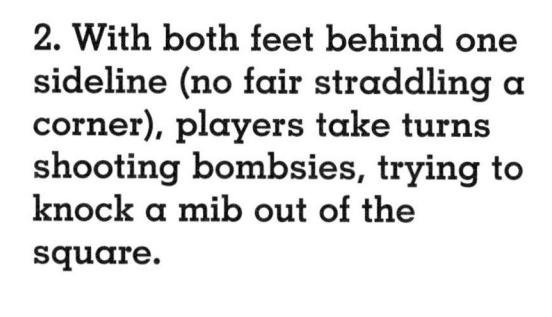
Object of game: To knock a mib out of the square by shooting bombsies

1. Instead of drawing a circle on the ground, draw a square, about three feet on each side. Each player puts in the same number of marbles (five or so) into the square.

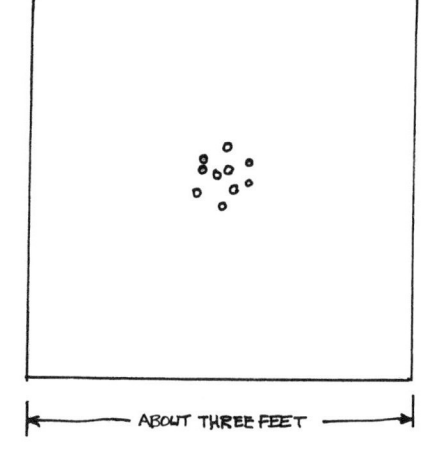

ABOUT THREE FEET

2. With both feet behind one sideline (no fair straddling a corner), players take turns shooting bombsies, trying to knock a mib out of the square.

3. If a player hits a mib out and his shooter rolls out of the square too, he gets to go again. Otherwise, his turn is over. At the end of a turn, a player picks up his shooter and keeps any marbles that he's knocked out of the square.

4. When all the mibs are gone, the game is over, and the player with the most marbles wins.

Variation:
Players try to hit a mib out of the square without letting the shooter leave too. If his shooter stays in the square, the player can go again; if not, his turn is over. Otherwise, the rules are the same.

OLD BOWLER
Abe Lincoln's favorite game—honestly!

Number of mibsters: Two or more
Difficulty:
Object of game: To hit the "old bowler" out of the square

1. Draw a square, then put one marble inside each corner and one in the center of the square. The marble in the middle is called the *old bowler.*

2. Draw a taw line somewhere outside the square (you can make it nearer or farther away, depending on how good you are).

MOVE IT **WAY** BACK!

TAW LINE

3. Players take turns standing behind the taw line and shooting at the mibs in the corners, trying to hit them out of the square. All four corner marbles must be hit out before players shoot at the old bowler.

4. Each player shoots until she misses a mib. If the old bowler is hit before all of the other mibs have been hit out (even if it's hit on a rebound from another shot), then the player who hit it is out of the game.

5. If a player's shooter hits a mib out of the square, that player keeps the mib and can shoot again from behind the taw line, regardless of where her shooter ended up.

6. If a player misses all the mibs and her shooter ends up inside the square, she must leave her shooter there to become another target. She may continue shooting on her next turn, with another shooter.

7. If a player misses all the mibs but her shooter leaves the square, she collects her shooter and shoots from behind the taw line on her next turn.

8. The game ends when the old bowler has been hit out. The player with the most marbles wins.

KNUCKLE BOX

Knuckle down in this square game from Brooklyn

Number of mibsters: Two or more

Difficulty: 🔴 🔴

Object of game: To hit a mib out of the square and keep your shooter inside it

1. Draw a square that is anywhere from eighteen inches to two feet on a side. Each player puts the same number of marbles in the square.

SHOOT ONE SPAN FROM SQUARE

2. Players take turns knuckling down at a one-span distance from the edge of the square (you can increase this to two or three spans, if you think you're good enough). The object is to hit a mib out of the square while keeping your shooter inside it.

3. If a player hits a mib out and his shooter rolls out of the square too, he keeps the mib, but his turn is over. If the shooter stays in, he keeps the mib and shoots again from outside the square, at a one-span distance.

4. If a player misses, he picks up his shooter and his turn is over.

5. When all the marbles have been shot out of the square, the player with the most marbles wins.

Variation:
Reverse the rules by having players try to make their shooter roll *out* of the square. Any shooter left in the square (whether or not a mib is knocked out) ends that player's turn; the shooter must remain there until that player's next turn. Until then, it is a fair target for other players.

SKELLY
Marbles really fly in this game

Number of mibsters: Two or more
Difficulty:
Object of game: To hit marbles so that they fly out of the square

1. Draw a square, then put one marble inside each corner and one in the center of the square. Draw a taw line ten feet away.

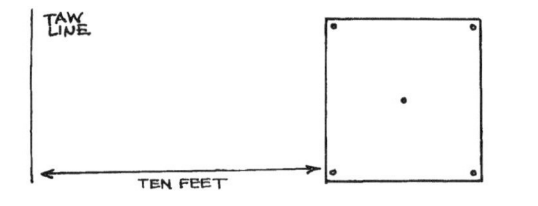

TAW LINE

TEN FEET

2. Players take turns shooting their marbles through the air from behind the taw line. They try to hit a mib so that it leaves the square in the air. You can stand when you shoot—you don't have to knuckle down.

TEN FEET

3. If a marble rolls rather than flies out of the square, it must be replaced at its original corner.

4. Each player gets one shot, whether she hits a mib out or not. After the shot, she collects her shooter and shoots on her next turn from behind the taw line.

5. The game is over when no mibs are left in the square.

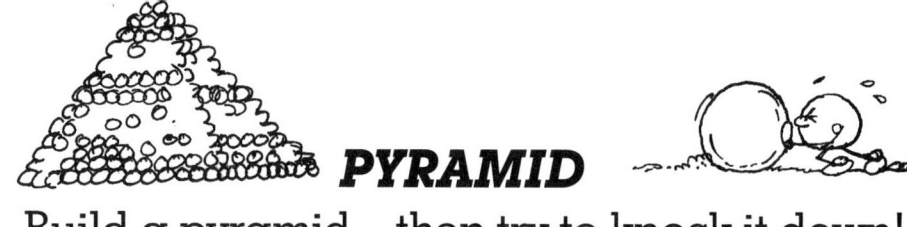

PYRAMID

Build a pyramid—then try to knock it down!

Number of mibsters: Two or more

Difficulty: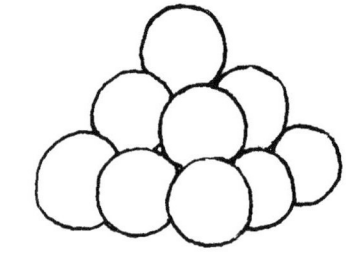

Object of game: To hit the pyramid and knock mibs out of the ring

1. The first player makes a pyramid out of thirteen marbles, as shown. He then draws a circle around the pyramid, about eighteen inches to two feet away from the pyramid. A few feet away from the edge of the circle, he draws a taw line.

2. The other players take turns shooting at the pyramid from anywhere behind the taw line, trying to knock a marble out of the ring.

3. If a player's shot misses, he pays the pyramid builder one marble and his turn is over.

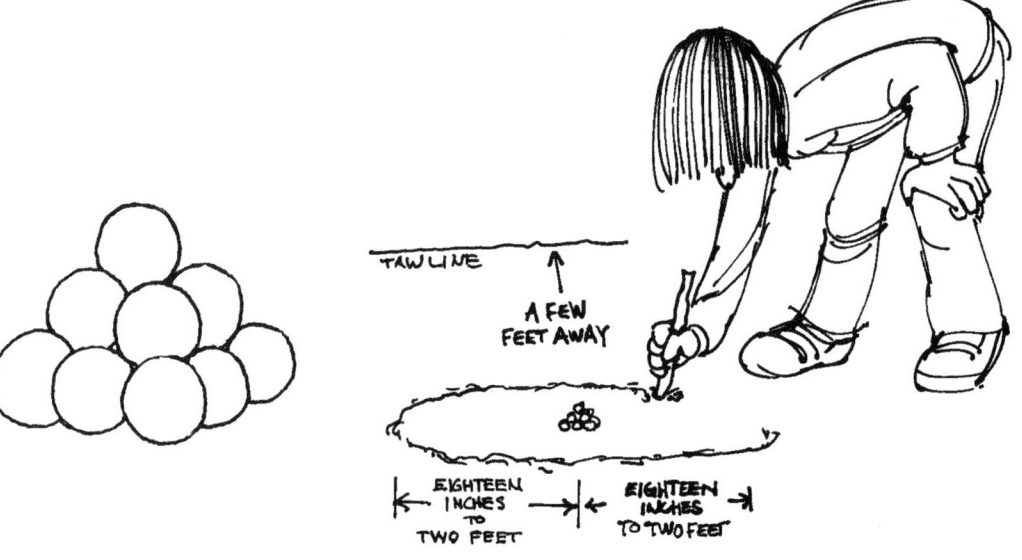

4. If the pyramid is hit but no mibs roll out, the pyramid builder restacks the pyramid and play continues with the next player. No fine is paid to the builder.

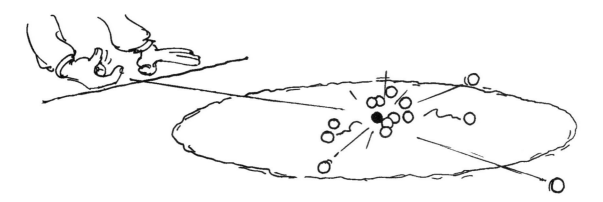

5. If a player hits the pyramid and knocks any mibs out, he keeps those that rolled out. He then becomes the new pyramid builder, and the game begins again.

Variation:

Instead of a pyramid (which risks thirteen marbles), the builder could make a triangle instead, as shown. This takes either six or ten marbles.

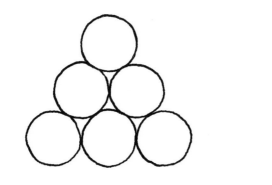

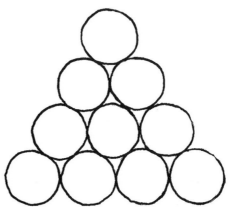

POISON CIRCLE
Stay out of the poison!

Number of mibsters: Two or more
Difficulty:
Object of game: To hit a mib out of the outer circle and stay away from the poison circle

1. Draw a circle on the ground, about seven feet across. Inside that circle, draw a smaller one (called the *poison circle*) one foot across. Each player puts the same number of marbles into the poison circle.

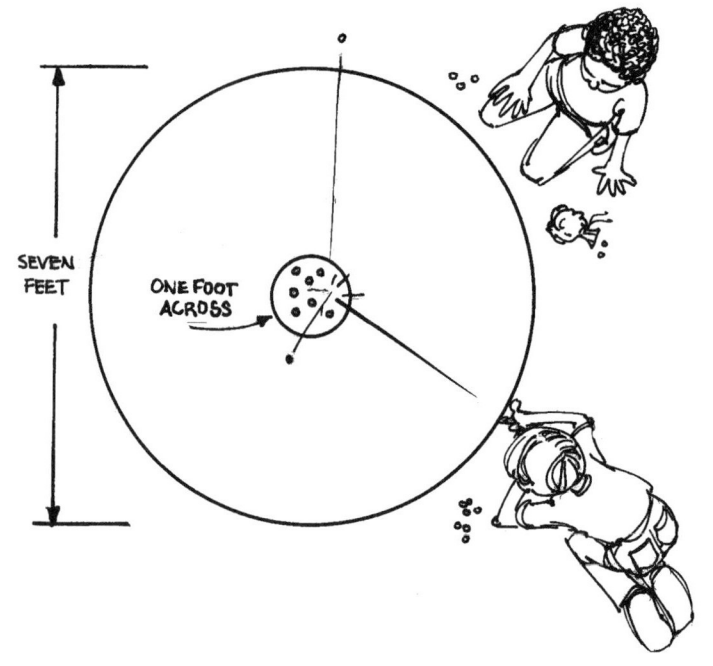

SEVEN FEET

ONE FOOT ACROSS

2. Players take turns trying to hit a mib out of both the poison circle and the outer circle. They try to keep their shooters out of the poison circle. No matter what happens, each player gets only one shot per turn and picks up her shooter at the end.

3. A player can keep a mib if she knocks it out of the large circle. If she misses or fails to knock a mib out, her turn is over.

4. If a player's shooter ends up in the poison circle, she must pay a marble into the poison circle to get her shooter back.

5. The game ends when the poison circle is empty.

POISON RING

Don't get hit by the poisoned marble!

Number of mibsters: Two
Difficulty: 🌀 🌍 🌐
Object of game: To get your shooter and one or more mibs out of the circle

1. Draw a circle on the ground, about five feet across. Inside that circle, draw a smaller one (the poison ring) one foot across. Each player puts four marbles into the poison ring.

2. Players take turns shooting at the marbles in the poison ring. Each player tries to end up with his shooter and one or more mibs outside the circle.

3. If a player misses, or if his shooter ends up inside the outer circle, he must put any marbles that rolled out back into the poison ring, along with all the marbles he has won so far in the game. If his shooter is inside the ring, it must remain there.

4. If a player succeeds in knocking his shooter and some mibs outside the ring, his shooter becomes "poisonous." On his next turn, he can shoot at the other player's shooters. If he hits one, that player is poisoned and must leave the game (keeping any marbles he won).

5. A player is poisoned until he misses another player's shooter or has to pay into the poison ring.

6. The game ends when the poison ring is empty, or when there is only one player left. He wins all the marbles in the poison ring.

FOOTBALL

America's two favorite games—together at last!

Number of mibsters: Two or more
Difficulty: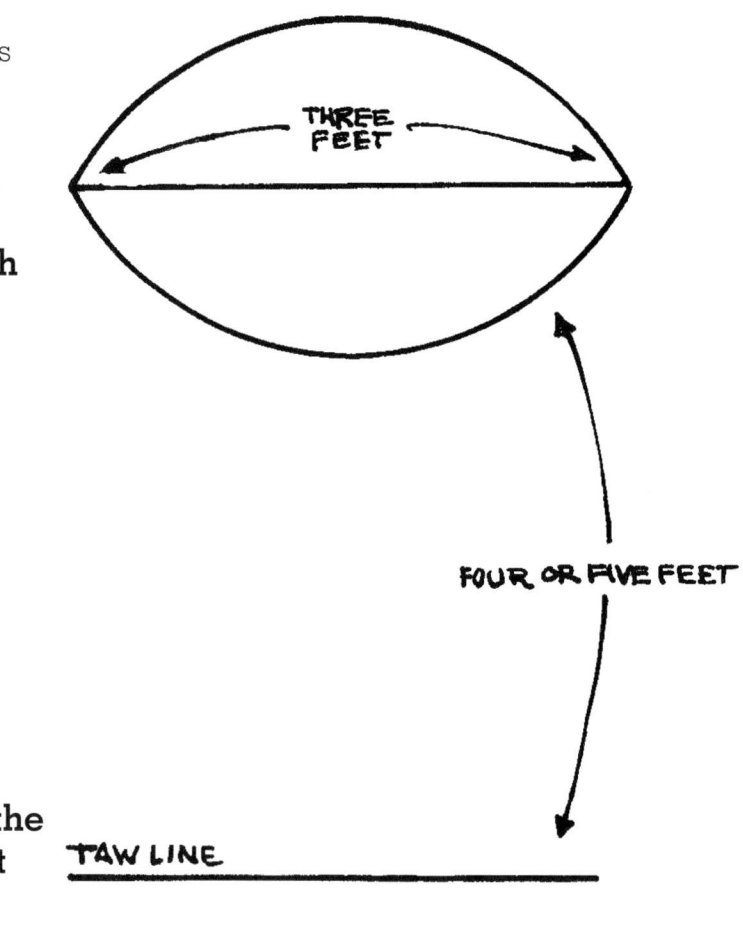
Object of game: To knock mibs
out of the football

1. Draw a football shape,
about three feet across,
and connect the ends with
a line, as shown. Draw a
taw line four or five feet
away.

2. Each player puts the
same number of marbles
on the line running
through the middle of
the football.

THREE FEET

FOUR OR FIVE FEET

TAW LINE

3. Players take turns
shooting from behind the
taw line, trying to knock the
mibs out of the football. It
doesn't matter where a
player's shooter ends up,
because she shoots from
behind the taw line every time.

4. If a mib rolls off the line but does not roll out of the football, it
is replaced on the line. A player keeps any mibs she knocks out
of the football.

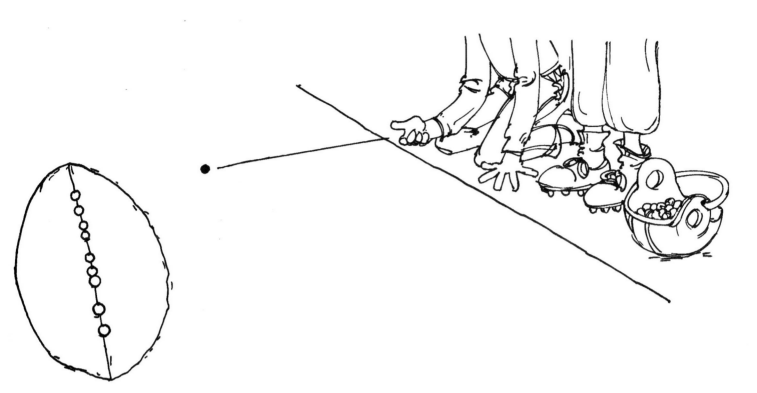

5. Each player gets one shot per turn, whether she hits a mib or not.

6. The game is over when all the mibs in the football have been claimed. The player with the most marbles wins.

Variations:

1. If a marble is hit off the line but does not leave the football, it is out of play and can be claimed by the player who contributed it.

2. If a player's shooter stops rolling inside the football, she may not reclaim it. It is placed on the line and becomes a target for other players.

NEWARK KILLER

One of you will become a killer—but which one?

Number of mibsters: Two or more

Difficulty: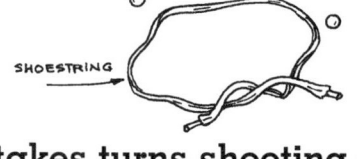

Object of game: To become the killer and win opponents' marbles

1. Make a circle on the ground with a shoelace, as shown. You can tie the ends or just leave them touching. Draw a taw line about ten feet away.

2. Each player gets ten marbles and takes turns shooting or rolling his marbles at the circle from behind the taw line. Some marbles will get knocked into the ring by other marbles and others will get knocked out of it.

3. The player who ends up with the most marbles in the ring becomes the "killer." He can shoot at any marbles outside the loop. If he hits one, he keeps it and continues shooting from where his shooter ends up. Once he misses, the game's over. All unclaimed marbles go back to their owners.

Variation:

A player becomes a "killer" after getting his marble into the ring. He can then shoot at other players' marbles from the taw line. If the "killer" hits another player's marble, that player is eliminated from the game, loses his shooter, and must pay the "killer" one marble. The "killer" can then continue shooting at other players' marbles (either from the edge of the ring or from where his shooter lies) until he misses. Once he misses, his turn is over and he is no longer a "killer."

HOLE GAMES
You won't believe you played the hole thing

Hole games are ideal for dirt surfaces, but you can play them elsewhere too. If you're inside or on a hard surface and you can't dig a hole, use a cup or a shoe instead. Marbles that hit the cup or shoe are considered to be "in the hole." Or you can lay the cup on its side and try to shoot into the cup. If you dig a hole, remember that the shallower the hole is, the harder it will be to get a marble to roll into it, so dig deep holes at first. Try to hit your marble in the *potty* or *puggy*, or shoot at a series of holes, as in Three Holes or Black Snake. Sometimes a hole is a good thing to hit, but sometimes you want to avoid it, as in Poison Pot. There's a "hole" lotta fun going on in these games!

NINE HOLES

Just as in golf, the lowest score wins

Number of mibsters: Two or more
Difficulty: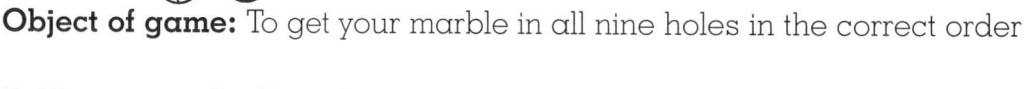
Object of game: To get your marble in all nine holes in the correct order

1. Dig nine shallow holes, about three inches across. The holes should make a backward *S*, as shown, and be about four feet apart.

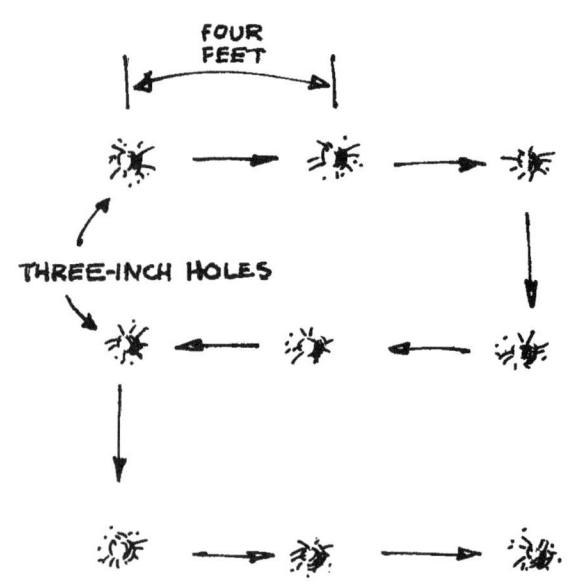

FOUR FEET

THREE-INCH HOLES

2. Players take turns shooting or throwing a shooter at the holes, trying to hit the holes in the order shown by the arrows in the diagram.

3. If a player gets her marble in the correct hole, she can shoot again at the next hole, standing at or behind the hole that her marble went into.

4. If a player misses a hole, or gets a marble in the incorrect hole, her turn is over, and she shoots on her next turn from wherever the marble ends up.

5. Keep track of the number of shots each player makes. The one to complete the course in the fewest number of shots wins.

Variations:

1. Draw a taw line a few feet before the first hole. When a player gets her shooter into a hole, she must take her next shot from behind the line. This makes the farther holes much harder to hit and can allow other players to catch up.

2. When a player gets her marble in the wrong hole, she must leave that marble in the hole. On her next turn, she shoots with a new marble from where she shot at the beginning of her last turn. The next player to correctly get her shooter in the hole with the "wrong" marble wins that marble.

PUGGY
Knock the marbles into the puggy

Number of mibsters: Two or more
Difficulty: 🔴 🔴
Object of game: To knock mibs—but not the shooter—into the puggy

1. Dig a small hole in the ground or draw a circle about six inches across. This hole is called the *puggy*. Draw a large circle (eight to ten feet across) around the puggy.

2. Each player drops the same number of marbles randomly inside the large circle (but not in the puggy).

PUGGY

SIX INCHES WIDE →

MAKE CIRCLE EIGHT TO TEN FEET WIDE

3. Players take turns shooting from outside the ring, trying to knock the mibs into the puggy. If a player succeeds, he keeps the mib, then shoots again from outside the circle.

4. If he doesn't hit any mibs into the hole, he picks up his shooter and shoots on his next turn from outside the circle.

5. If a player's shooter rolls into the hole, he cannot keep any mibs that he knocked out of the circle, and his turn is over. He may retrieve his shooter, however.

6. The game is over when no mibs are left in the ring. The player with the most marbles is the winner.

Variation:
Players who do not hit a mib in the hole must leave their shooters where they stop rolling. On their next turn, they shoot from anywhere outside the circle. But when a player hits a mib into the hole, he becomes a "killer," and can then shoot at the shooters of other players. If the "killer" hits a player's shooter, that player must pay the "killer" one marble, and the "killer" gets another shot. A player remains the "killer" until he misses.

POTTY

It takes a lot of training to win this game!

Number of mibsters: Two or more

Difficulty:

Object of game: To get your shooter into the potty and collect the other players' marbles

1. Dig a shallow hole about one inch across to be the "potty." Draw a taw line about five to ten feet away. You can lag for first by throwing marbles at the potty from the taw line. The player whose marble gets closest to the potty without going in gets to go first.

POTTY
ONE INCH
HOLE

FIVE TO TEN
FEET FROM
TAW TO HOLE

TAW LINE

2. The first player shoots from behind the taw line and tries to get her shooter into the potty. If she succeeds, every other player must give her one marble, and the game starts over.

3. If the first player misses, then the other players take turns shooting into the potty. The first one to get a marble in can collect all marbles within a span of the potty.

4. Before she collects the marbles, however, the next player has three shots to hit her marble into the potty. You can decide if you want to shoot from behind the line or (especially if you're playing with a cup or a shoe) from above, by bombsies.

5. If the next player hits her marble, that player collects the marbles within a span of the potty instead. Otherwise, the first player can take the marbles. Then the game begins again.

Variations:
1. Instead of the next player being allowed a chance to shoot at the first player's marble (and steal her winnings), the first player collects her winnings and waits while play continues among the other players.

2. The first player into the potty can swap out her marble to make it harder for the next player to hit it. In other words, she can put in a peewee instead of a larger marble. But the next player can also change to a bigger marble, to hit the first player's marble more easily.

POISON POT
Try to get poisoned and win all the marbles!

Number of mibsters: Two or more
Difficulty: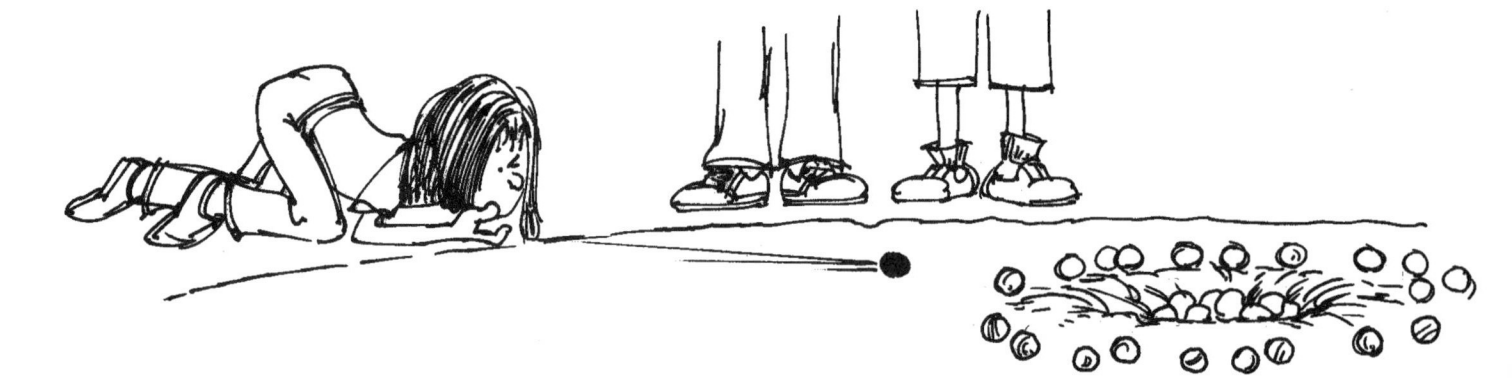
Object of game: To shoot mibs out of the outer circle and stay out of the "poison pot"

1. Dig a small, shallow hole six to eight inches across or draw a circle the same size. This is the *poison pot*. Surround the poison pot with a larger circle, less than five feet across.

2. Each player contributes one marble to the poison pot and the same number of marbles (two or three is good) to the ring around the pot.

3. Taking turns, each player shoots from anywhere along the outer circle, trying to hit a mib out of the ring. The shooter should leave the circle too. Don't shoot at the marbles in the poison pot.

4. If a player hits both a marble and his shooter out of the circle, he keeps the marble and shoots again from anywhere outside the circle.

5. If a player misses a marble or leaves his shooter inside the poison pot, he must pay all the marbles he's won so far into the poison pot, and his turn is over. If he has not won any marbles yet, he must pay two marbles into the poison pot.

6. Play continues until one player wins ten marbles. If there are no mibs in the circle before this happens, put all the marbles back and start again.

7. Once a player has won ten marbles, he is "poison" and can try to win the other players' marbles. The poison player splits all the marbles he has won among the other players, and everyone collects the mibs still in the ring that belong to them.

8. The player who shot after the poison player must put all of the marbles he won in the game (including the ones just given to him) into a circle around the poison pot. The poison player then shoots at these marbles, keeping any marbles that he hits out of the ring, until he fails to hit a marble out. The other player collects any of his marbles still in the circle.

9. Each player, in turn, does the same, and the poison player has a chance to win all the marbles. The game is over when the poison player has had a chance to shoot at every player's marbles.

Variation:
For a shorter game, reduce the number of marbles required for a player to be "poison."

THREE HOLES
A favorite around the world

Number of mibsters: Two or more (sometimes two teams)
Difficulty:
Object of game: To get a marble into each of the three holes in a particular order

1. Begin the game by digging three shallow holes, each about three inches across. The holes should be about ten feet apart. Draw a taw line ten feet from the first hole.

TAW LINE

TEN FEET FROM TAW TO HOLE!

THREE INCHES WIDE

2. The object of the game is to get a marble in each of the three holes in a particular order. You can begin by hitting them 1-2-3, but some rules require you to hit them 2-3-2-1, or hitting them 1-2-3 three times in a row. You and your friends can invent your own order!

3. Players take turns standing behind the taw line and shooting at the first hole. Knuckling down is not required, and tossing a marble is allowed.

4. A player gets an extra shot if her marble ends up in the correct hole or if she hits another player's marble. It's a good strategy, then, to hit other players' marbles away from a hole if they're near one. Marbles are shot on the next turn from where they stop rolling.

5. The first player to land in all the holes in the correct order is the winner.

Variations:

1. Killer Three Holes (played in England): After entering the first hole, a player hitting another player's marble collects a penalty from that player (usually one marble). Another option is to eliminate a player whose marble has been hit from the game.

2. Rolley Hole (played in the United States): Players shoot in teams (usually two teams of two), and each team tries to get one member's marbles in the holes. With teams, the three-hole course is often run several times. Spanning is also allowed, so that a marble rolling within a span of a hole is considered in. A player cannot span her marble to hit another player's marble, however.

3. Nucks (played in Australia): Players can span to enter a hole and span to leave it (by shooting a span away from the edge of the hole). Players can "kill" other players, as in variation 1, but only after they've gotten their marble in all three holes.

HUNDREDS

First player to one hundred wins!

Number of mibsters: Two
Difficulty:
Object of game: To collect one hundred points

1. Dig a shallow hole, about eight to ten inches across, and draw a taw line about ten to fifteen feet away.

2. Players take turns shooting at the hole from behind the line. Each time only one player shoots a marble into the hole, that player gets ten points. Each player gets only one shot per turn, regardless of whether or not points are earned.

3. If both players, or neither one, make it into the hole, neither player gets any points and both shoot again from behind the line.

4. The first player to one hundred points wins.

Variations:
1. If one player misses the hole on his shot, he must leave his shooter where it stops rolling. The next player may shoot at the hole or at the other player's shooter. If he hits the shooter, he earns ten points, and the other player loses ten points.

2. Getting a marble in the hole (or hitting another player's marble) earns that player another turn.

HIT THE SPOT

Three times is the charm

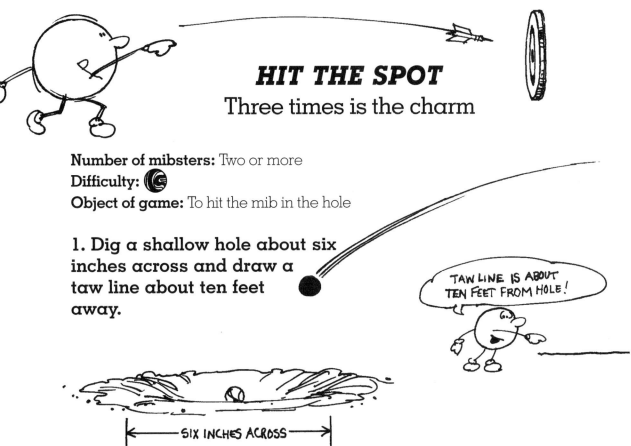

Number of mibsters: Two or more
Difficulty:
Object of game: To hit the mib in the hole

1. Dig a shallow hole about six inches across and draw a taw line about ten feet away.

TAW LINE IS ABOUT TEN FEET FROM HOLE!

SIX INCHES ACROSS

2. One player puts a marble in the hole to serve as a mib. Each player takes turns shooting or tossing a marble from behind the line, trying to hit the mib in the hole.

3. If a player misses the mib, she shoots on her next turn from wherever her marble ends up. If she hits the mib, she shoots from behind the line on her next turn. Each turn consists of only one shot, regardless of whether or not the mib is hit.

4. When a player has hit the mib three times, she wins the mib, along with any other marbles on the ground.

5. A new player puts a marble into the hole, and play begins again. The game continues until each player has put a mib into the hole. The player with the most marbles wins.

BLACK SNAKE
Don't get bitten by the snake!

Number of mibsters: Two or more

Difficulty:

Object of game: To become a "black snake" by successfully navigating the course

1. Dig a series of seven holes at different distances from one another to make the course. The holes shouldn't be in a line and can be different sizes and depths. See the diagram for one way that the holes can be arranged.

2. Players take turns shooting at the holes in order (see arrows).

3. If a player gets a marble into the proper hole, he earns another shot and continues his turn by shooting from any spot within a span of the hole. Players who miss shoot from wherever their marbles end up.

4. When he's shot his marble into all seven holes, a player shoots at all seven in reverse order, going backward through the course.

5. Once a player has made it through all seven holes twice, he becomes a "black snake" and shoots at other players' marbles. There is no limit to the number of black snakes allowed in a game.

6. If a black snake hits another player's shooter, that player is eliminated from the game. However, if a black snake shoots his shooter into a hole, he himself is eliminated.

7. The winner is the last player to remain in the game.

Variation:
If you're playing on a hard surface or just want a different kind of game, use everyday objects like tennis shoes, cups, trash cans, or books instead of holes. A marble is considered in as long as it hits that object, and players continue shooting from wherever the marble stops rolling.

HANDERS
No off-the-wall shots allowed

Number of mibsters: Two or more
Difficulty:
Object of game: To throw a handful of marbles into the hole

1. Dig a small hole about one foot from a wall, and draw a taw line about five to ten feet from the wall.

2. Decide who goes first by lagging toward the hole. The closest player to the hole goes first, followed by the second closest, and so forth. Going first is a tremendous advantage, as you will see.

3. Everyone contributes two marbles to the first player, who stands behind the taw line and throws all the marbles toward the hole at the same time.

4. The first player keeps any marbles that end up in the hole, except for those marbles that hit the wall first.

5. The second player collects all the marbles remaining to be won and, standing behind the taw line, throws them at the hole. She wins marbles as the first player did.

6. Play continues in this fashion until all the marbles have been won. Then everyone contributes two more marbles, and the second player throws first.

7. The game is over when everyone has had a chance to throw first.

CORONA

Step right up and take a chance!

Number of mibsters: Two or more

Difficulty:

Object of game: To drop a marble into the hole in the corona

1. A cigar box, shoe box, or any box with a lid will do to make the corona. Cut a hole about two inches in diameter in the lid of the corona.

2. One player runs the corona, winning the marbles of the losers and paying marbles to the winner. Each of the other players takes turns shooting bombsies, trying to drop a marble into the hole in the corona.

3. The player who runs the corona decides what the prize is for each player, depending on how tall that player is (and therefore how far away he is from the hole). The prize is usually five to ten marbles, although it could also be a particularly valuable marble. Each player must know what his prize will be before he shoots.

4. Winners are paid the promised prize, while losers must give their marble to the corona keeper. For obvious reasons, this is a game that must be played for keeps.

5. The game continues until everyone has taken a shot at the corona, or as many shots as they want to take. Then another player becomes the keeper of the corona, and the game begins again.

SHOOTING GAMES

No more props—these games are for true marble fans

When you're done shooting at holes or in circles, try these games. They're the game of marbles at its simplest, where all you have to do is shoot. But you'd better learn to be a good shooter first. Sometimes you'll have to shoot bombsies, plunk, or knuckle down to make your shot. These games will test the strongest and most accurate of thumbs to the limit. Be careful, too, because some of these games can only be played keepsies. They're a good way to win a lot of marbles, but also a good way to lose all the marbles in your precious marble bag. There are a few games with props— Boxies and Die Shot—but they still depend on a good shooter's eye and concentration.

BOSS OUT

Keep chasing the "boss"—but don't get hit!

Number of mibsters: Two or more
Difficulty: 🔮 🔮
Object of game: To hit the boss

1. One player puts down a marble to be the target, called the "boss." Mark off a shooting line about ten feet away from the boss.

2. Players take turns shooting at the boss. The first player to hit the boss gets to keep it and collect her shooter. The other players collect their marbles and start the game over again, with the next player putting down a boss.

3. If all players have shot once and no one has hit the boss, everyone whose marble landed within a giant step of the boss can try to hit it by shooting bombsies. The closest player shoots first, and those players who are farther away than one giant step pick up their marbles.

4. The first player to hit the boss shooting bombsies wins the boss and all marbles still on the ground. Start the game again by having the next player put down a boss.

5. If nobody is within a giant step, or nobody hits the marble, the round starts again, with everyone shooting at the same target.

6. The game continues until every player has put down a boss. The player with the most marbles wins.

BOUNCE ABOUT
Like Boss Out, but the stakes are higher

Number of mibsters: Two or more, but more is better
Difficulty:
Object of game: To hit the first player's shooter

1. Draw a taw line. The first player rolls his marble a good distance from the taw line to be a target.

2. The next player tries to hit the first player's marble, either by shooting or rolling his shooter. If he hits it, he keeps the target, then tosses out one of his own, and play continues with the next player.

3. Each player can shoot at any marble that has been rolled out, whether or not it is the original target marble. If a player hits more than one marble, he may keep them all.

4. The game is over when everyone has taken a turn and missed. All the players collect their marbles from the ground, and the player with the most marbles wins.

Variation:
Because some players might not want to shoot with (and risk losing) their best shooter, try this variation. A player who hits another player's marble does not keep that marble but collects a one-marble penalty from the player he hit.

PICKING PLUMS

Pick a marble off the line and it's yours

Number of mibsters: Two or more
Difficulty:
Object of game: To hit a mib off the line

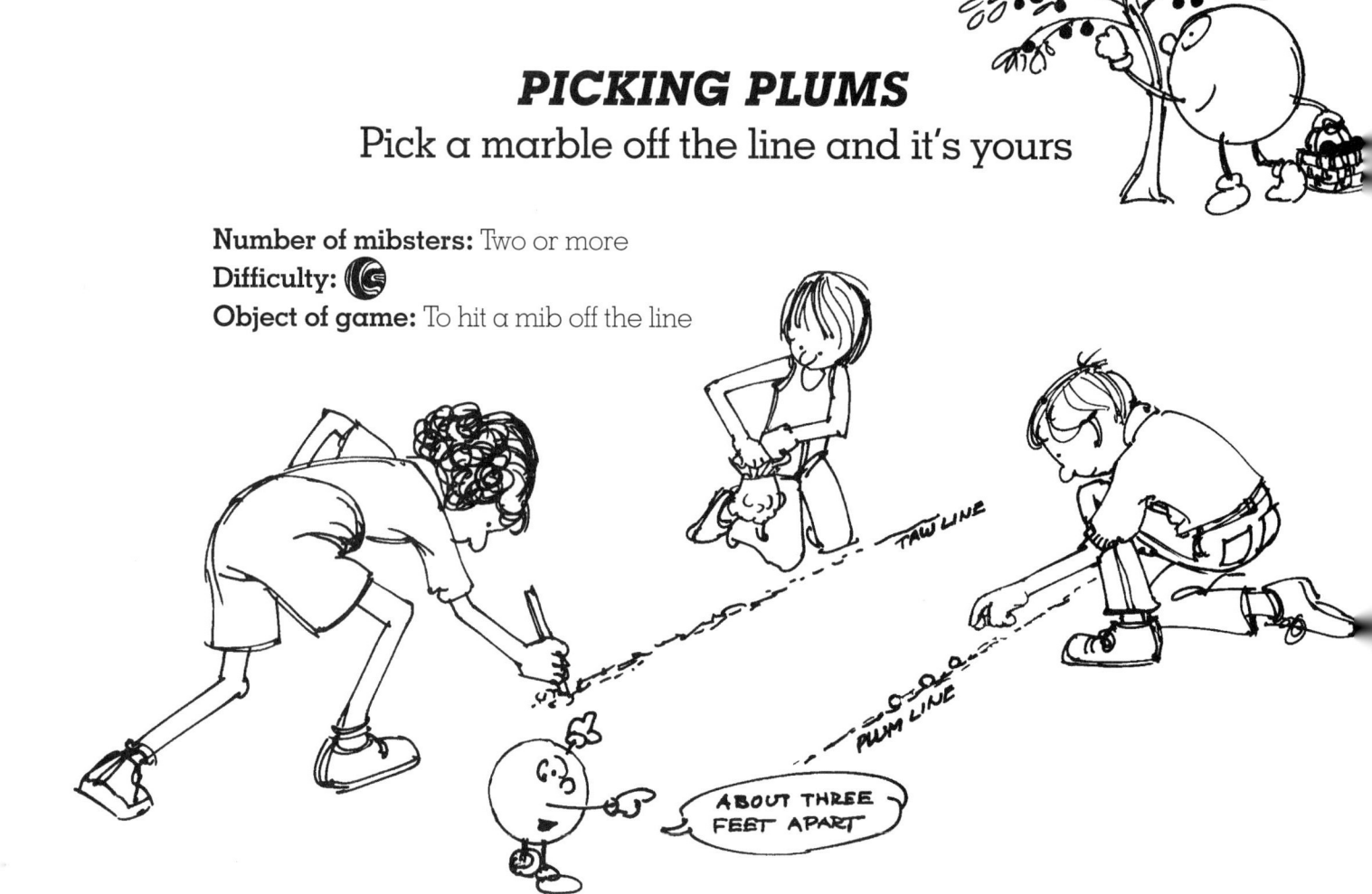

TAW LINE

PLUM LINE

ABOUT THREE FEET APART

1. Start by drawing two parallel lines about three feet apart. One line is the plum line and the other is the taw line.

2. Each player contributes four marbles and places them on the plum line. The mibs should be about two marble-widths apart.

3. Each player takes turns shooting at the mibs on the plum line while standing behind the taw line.

4. If a player hits a mib off the line, she gets to keep that marble.

5. There's only one shot per turn, and every shot is taken from behind the taw line, regardless of where a player's shooter ends up or whether she hits a mib.

6. The game is over when all the mibs have been hit off the line. The player with the most marbles wins.

Variations:

1. Picking Plums can be played in two teams, with each team contributing the same number of marbles. Two taw lines are drawn, one for each team, on either side of the plum line. Each team's marbles are placed on the side of the plum line farthest from their own taw line. Each team then gets three shots per turn (one player per turn) from behind the taw line, trying to hit one of the other team's marbles across the plum line. Between turns, each team collects its three shooters, as well as the marbles won in that turn. The first team to hit all of the opposing team's marbles across the plum line wins.

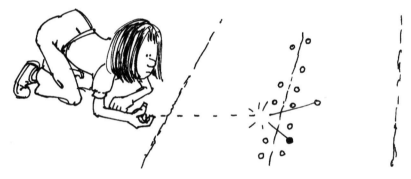

2. In Dobblers, a player who misses a mib must leave her shooter where it ends up. If another player hits her shooter, she must add another marble to the plum line. Shots are still always taken from behind the taw line.

3. In One Step, players take their first shot standing up, either bombsies or by taking a step, then tossing the marble. In both shots, players must remain behind the taw line. Every other shot is taken from behind the line, except if a player hits a mib off the line. In that case, an extra shot is earned, taken from wherever the shooter stops rolling.

HIT AND SPAN
Be careful how you shoot, Jack

Number of mibsters: Two or more
Difficulty: 🔘
Object of game: To hit the jack or get within a span of it

TAW LINE

1. Draw a taw line. From behind the taw line, the first player tosses out a marble to be a *jack*.

2. Players take turns shooting at the jack from behind the taw line.

3. If a player hits the jack or gets within a span of it, he gets to keep the jack, along with all the other marbles on the ground. The next player tosses out a marble to be the new jack.

4. Each time a player misses, his shooter becomes the new jack, and the next player shoots at it from behind the taw line.

5. The game continues until everyone has tossed out a jack, or until a certain number of marbles are won.

BOMBERS
Hit and Span with a twist for two

Number of mibsters: Two
Difficulty: 🪀 🪀
Object of game: To hit the other player's jack

1. Draw a taw line. The first player rolls out a marble to be the jack.

2. The second player then shoots at the jack from behind the taw line. If she misses it, the first player picks up her jack and the second player rolls out a new jack. But if she hits the first player's jack, she keeps it and the first player must roll out a new jack.

3. The second player shoots again at this new jack, this time standing next to it and shooting bombsies. If she hits it, she keeps this jack too.

4. Whether or not she hits the new jack, the second player rolls out a marble to be the jack and the first player gets a chance to shoot at it, continuing as in step 2.

5. The game is over when one player has won ten marbles.

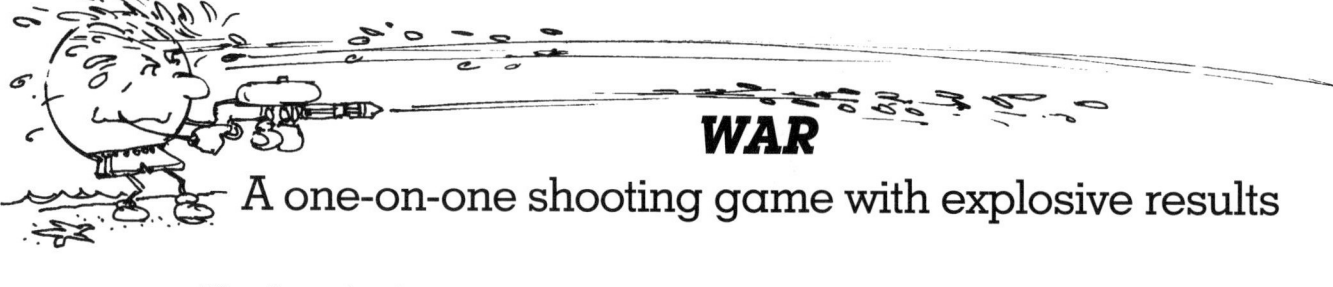

WAR

A one-on-one shooting game with explosive results

Number of mibsters: Two
Difficulty: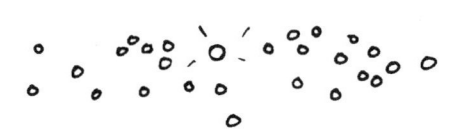
Object of game: To hit the target marble

1. Draw a taw line. One player rolls out a marble to be a target.

2. The second player stands behind the taw line and tries to hit the target marble. Each time he misses, he must pay the first player one marble.

3. When he hits the target, the second player keeps it and rolls out a marble to be a target for the first player. The game continues as in step 2.

4. Marbles can change hands quickly and in large numbers in this game, so be careful about playing this one for keeps. The game often ends when one player runs out of marbles, but you can set a certain number of marbles as a goal for the winner. The game is over when one player reaches that goal, and he is the winner.

TAW LINE

STICKER

Whoever owns the sticker could win big—or lose big

Number of mibsters: Two or more
Difficulty: 🔘
Object of game: To hit the sticker

1. Traditionally, this game is begun by the first person to shout "Sticker!" We recommend that you take turns, however, to give everyone a chance.

2. One player places a marble (the *sticker*) on a smooth rolling surface and draws a taw line ten or fifteen feet away. Since this game is played for keeps, the sticker should be an especially precious marble, valuable enough for other players to risk their shooters.

3. Other players take turns shooting at the sticker from behind the taw line. The first player to hit the sticker wins it. When a player misses, she loses her marble to the owner of the sticker.

4. The game continues until everyone's had a shot at the sticker, or until someone wins it. Then someone else offers a sticker, and the game starts over.

MARBLE ARCH
One of the oldest marble games

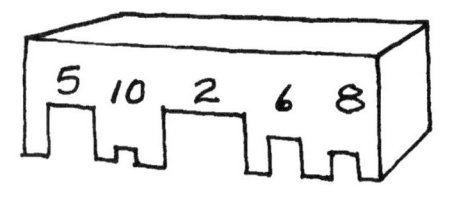

Number of mibsters: Two or more
Difficulty:
Object of game: To roll a marble through one of the holes

1. Take a small box (like a shoe box or cigar box) and cut square holes in the side to make your Marble Arch, as shown in the diagram. You can make some holes smaller, so it's harder to roll a marble through them. Mark a number between one and ten above each hole. If you've made some holes smaller than others, you should mark higher numbers above them.

2. Choose one player to be the arch keeper. He sets up the Marble Arch and draws a taw line five to ten feet away.

3. Players take turns trying to roll a marble through one of the holes from behind the taw line. Marbles are picked up after

each shot. For each missed shot, that player must pay the arch keeper one marble.

4. If a player rolls a marble through one of the holes, the arch keeper must pay that player as many marbles as the number above the hole indicates.

5. The game continues until everyone has had five shots. Then a new player becomes the arch keeper.

Variations:

1. If you'd rather not sacrifice marbles, set a winning score that everyone tries to reach. In this game, there is no arch keeper and therefore no penalty for missing a hole. Players simply take turns rolling a marble, winning the number of points indicated above each hole that their marble passes through. The first player to reach the winning score is the winner.

2. Another way to play without an arch keeper is to have players leave their marbles wherever they stop rolling, shooting with a new marble at each turn. When a player makes it through a hole, he collects his winnings from the marbles on the ground. The game ends when all the marbles on the ground have been won.

3. Make a matching set of holes on the other side of the box. Only those marbles that roll all the way through the box (through both holes) earn the points. You can also mark the holes with even numbers, and give players half the score when they get their marble through the first hole.

4. Poison Arches: Players use only one shooter and leave missed marbles where they stop rolling. If his marble is hit by another player, the player whose marble is hit must pay the other player one marble. However, if another player knocks his marble through a hole, the player whose marble was hit collects the designated number of marbles from the player who hit it (not from the arch keeper).

OFF THE WALL
This game's not as crazy as it sounds

Number of mibsters: Two or more
Difficulty: 🔴 🔴
Object of game: To bounce your marble off the wall and hit the mib

1. Mark off a taw line five to ten feet away from a wall.

2. The first player throws a marble against the wall to serve as a mib.

3. On each first shot, players aim at the mib from behind the taw line. Before it hits the mib, though, the shooter must rebound off the wall.

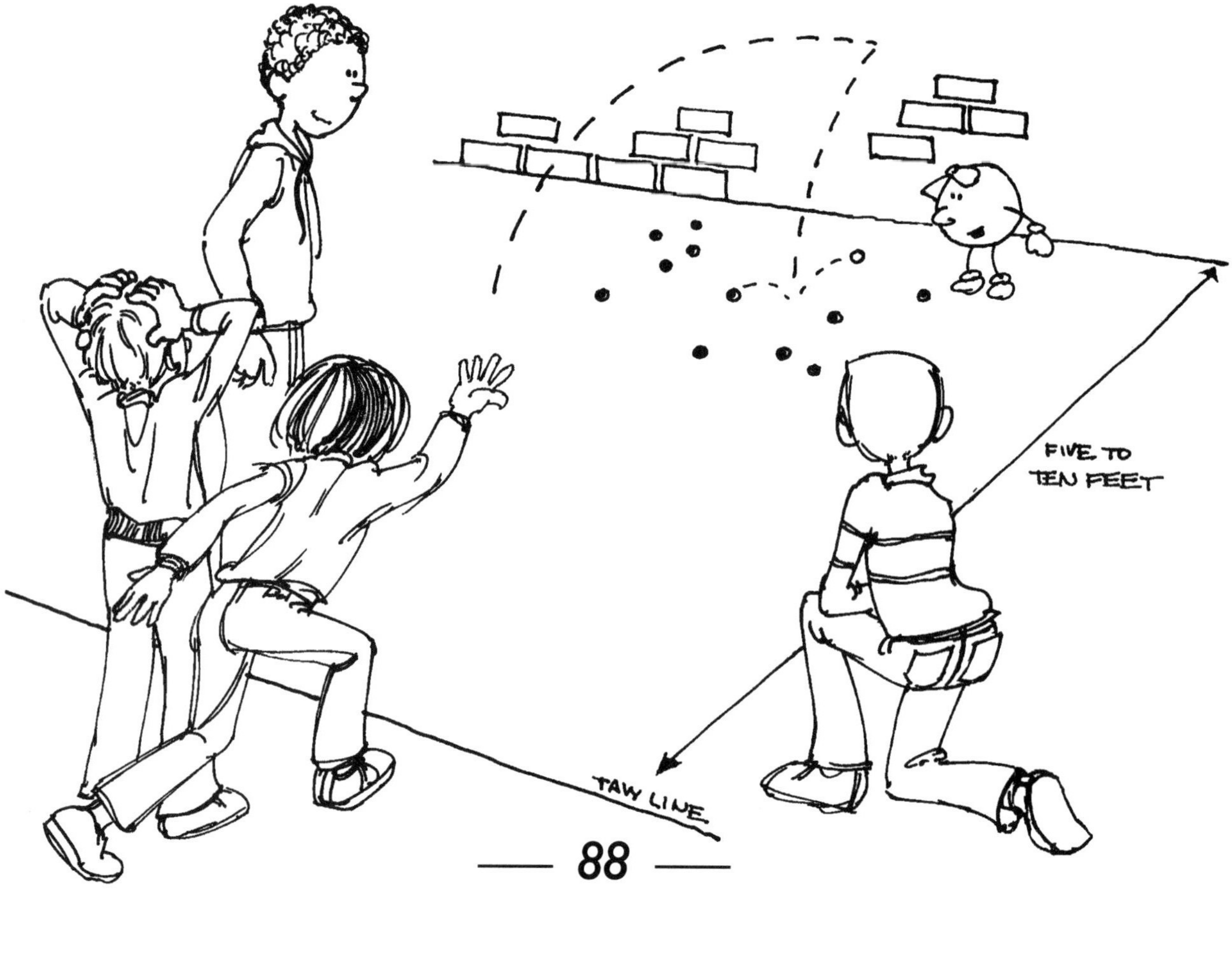

FIVE TO TEN FEET

TAW LINE

4. If a player misses the mib, she leaves her marble where it lands.

5. If a player hits the mib, she collects it along with all the marbles on the ground. She then throws out a new mib, and the game continues.

6. If all the players have taken their first shot and none of them has hit the mib, the game continues, but each player shoots her marble from wherever it landed on the last turn.

7. The game is over when one player wins ten marbles.

Variation:
When all the players have shot and missed, any marble between the wall and the line is a mib. Players still shoot in order, from where their marbles lie, but hitting a mib only wins a player that one marble. The game continues until all of the marbles are gone.

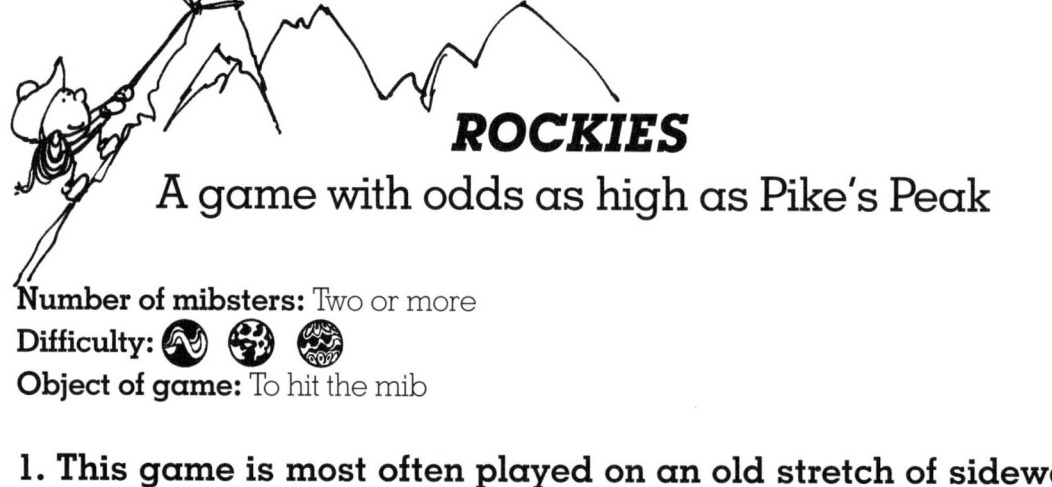

ROCKIES
A game with odds as high as Pike's Peak

Number of mibsters: Two or more
Difficulty: 🌀 🌐 🌀
Object of game: To hit the mib

1. This game is most often played on an old stretch of sidewalk, but you can make up your own difficult course wherever you can find the room. The idea is to find the bumpiest, crackiest, most uneven area possible, then put a mib in the hardest place to reach.

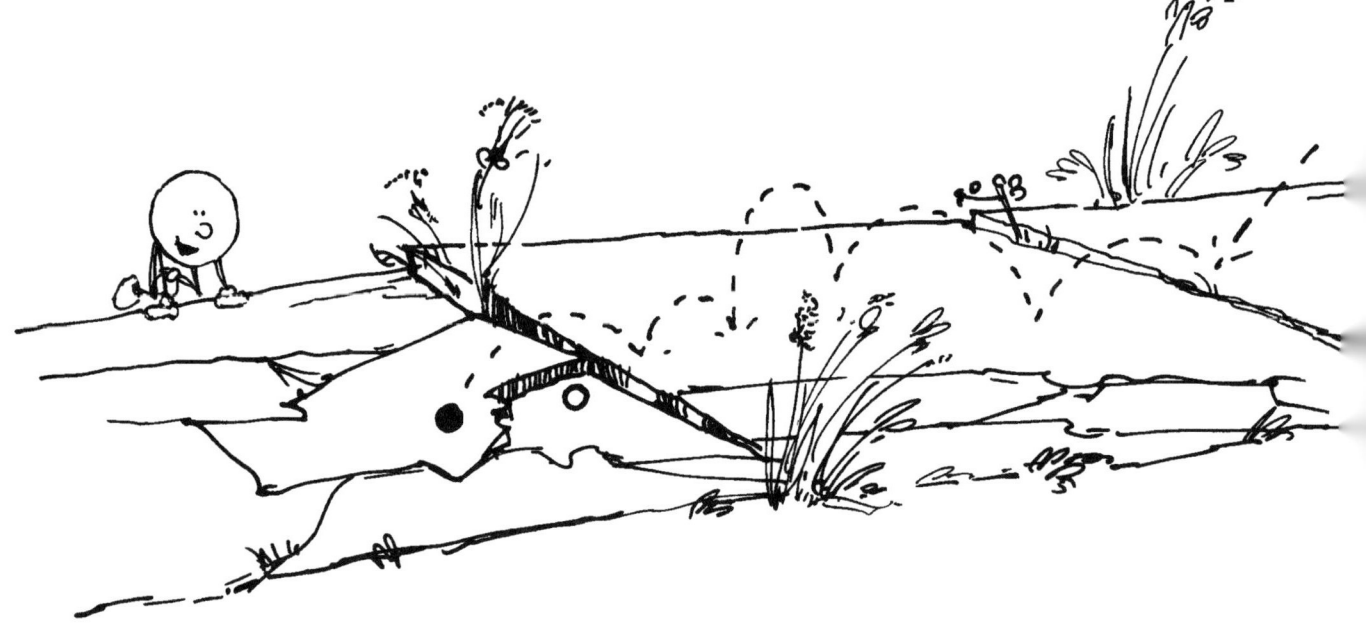

2. The person to find and make the course is in charge of the mib, although you can rotate this duty if you want to. Players take turns shooting at the mib, losing their shooters if they miss, which almost everyone will.

3. The lucky—or skilled—shooter who manages to hit the mib collects fifty marbles from the player in charge of the mib. (Now you can see why the course has to be so hard!)

4. The game ends when someone hits the mib, or when all the players get sick of losing their marbles, whichever comes first!

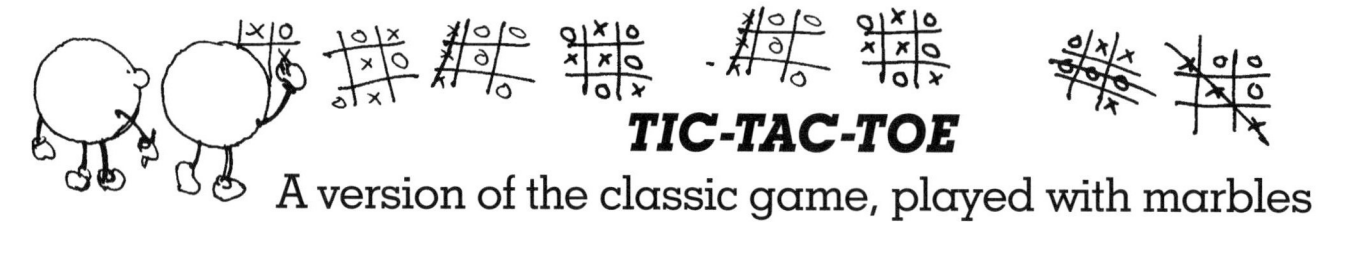

TIC-TAC-TOE

A version of the classic game, played with marbles

Number of mibsters: Two
Difficulty: ⊛ ⊛ ⊛
Object of game: To get three marbles in a row

1. Draw a tic-tac-toe diagram on the ground or sidewalk, making the squares about two feet or so on each side. Better players can play on a smaller diagram, and new players might want to make the diagram bigger. Draw a taw line five to ten feet away.

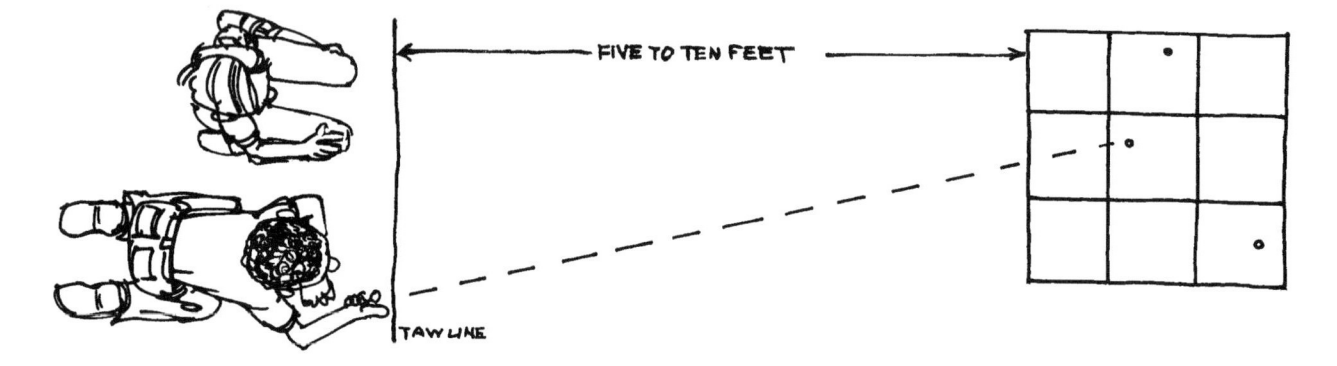

FIVE TO TEN FEET

TAW LINE

2. The players take turns shooting from behind the taw line. As in the pencil version, this game calls for players to get three of their marbles in a row, horizontally, vertically, or diagonally. To make it easier to tell the two players' marbles apart, each person should try to use a different kind or color of marble.

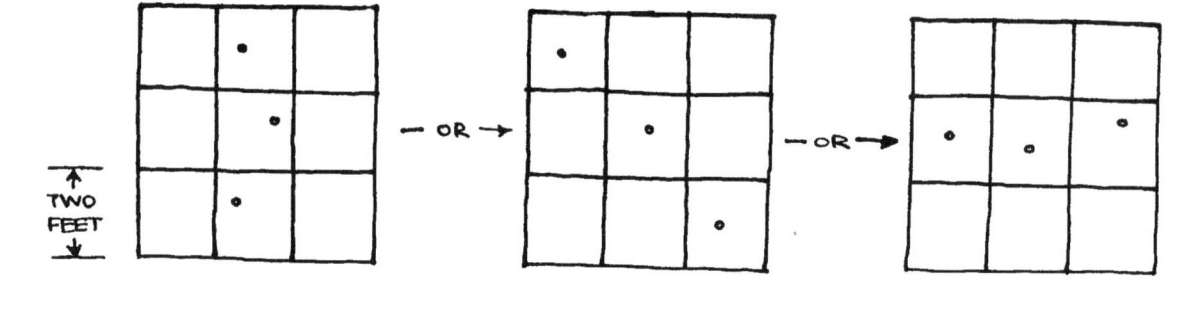

TWO FEET

— OR →   — OR →

3. Each player gets only one shot per turn, no matter where her marble ends up. Marbles that don't end up on a square should be picked up.

4. The first marble in a square occupies that square, and the only way to win that square back is to knock the marble out. Any marble that ends up in the same square as another marble without knocking the marble out must be picked up.

5. The first player to get three of her marbles in a row is the winner. If you play for keeps, then she collects all the marbles in the squares.

6. There are no tie games in marble tic-tac-toe. If all the squares are filled up but there's no winner (or if all the winning rows are blocked), keep on shooting, trying to knock the other player's marble out of the way. The game doesn't stop until there's a winner.

Variation:

1. For a tougher tic-tac-toe-*toe* game, make your diagram four squares by four squares. The object is still to make three marbles in a row, but there are now more ways to do it. Otherwise, the rules are the same.

2. Experts can try this version of the game: Use the tic-tac-toe-toe diagram, but try to get four marbles in a row. With great shooters, this game is either over in a few minutes—or it lasts a few hours!

BOXIES

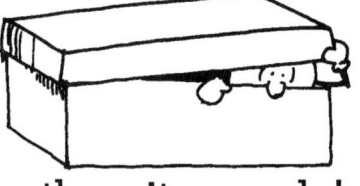

Roll a marble in the box—it's harder than it sounds!

Number of mibsters: Two or more
Difficulty: 🌀 🌐 🌀
Object of game: To roll a marble into the box and make it stay there

1. The best kind of box for this game is a cigar box, because it has a lid that you can use as a ramp. Any kind of box will do, though. See the diagrams here for suggestions as to how to angle your box. The idea is to make it difficult (but not impossible) for a marble to roll into the box and stay there. Draw a taw line about ten to twenty feet away from the box.

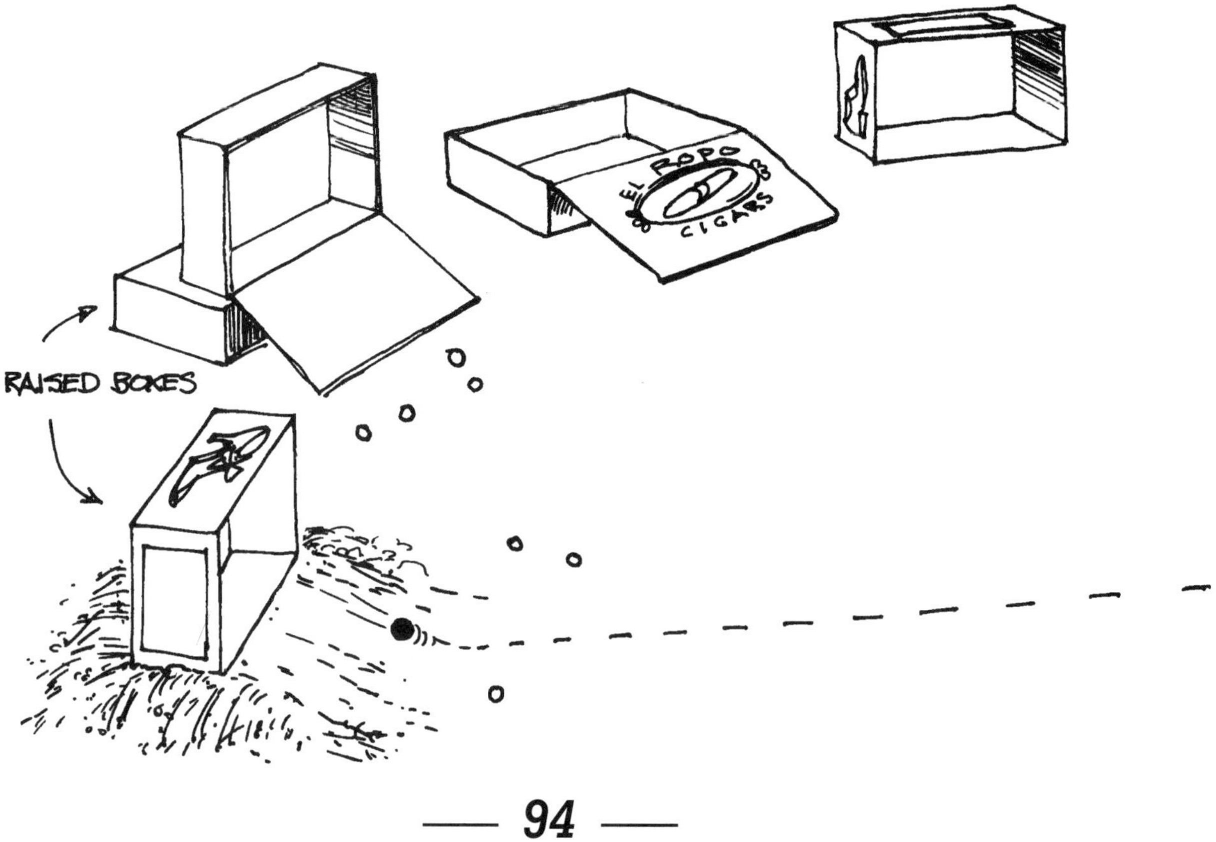

RAISED BOXES

2. Players take turns rolling a marble from behind the taw line, trying to get it to stay in the box. Marbles that roll in the box but then roll back out again don't count. Players who miss collect their marbles and shoot on their next turn from behind the taw line.

3. The first player to roll a marble into the box and make it stay there wins.

Variations:

1. Appoint one player to be the box keeper. Any marbles that don't stay in the box go to the box keeper. But anyone who gets a marble to stay in the box collects five marbles from the box keeper.

2. Instead of appointing a box keeper, you can play that the player who gets a marble to stay in the box wins all the marbles on the ground (or five of them, if you don't want to be greedy).

TEN TO TWENTY FEET!

TAW LINE

DIE SHOT
Win one to six marbles—or lose your shooter

Number of mibsters: Two or more
Difficulty: 🔵 🔵
Object of game: To knock the die off the marble

1. Take a die and balance it on top of a marble, as shown. If you have trouble getting the die to stay, you can press the marble into the dirt or gravel to stop it from rolling. If this doesn't work, you can rub the marble on the sidewalk (or rub it with a rough file) to make opposite sides flat. Don't use a favorite or valuable marble, since it won't be good for any other game but Die Shot.

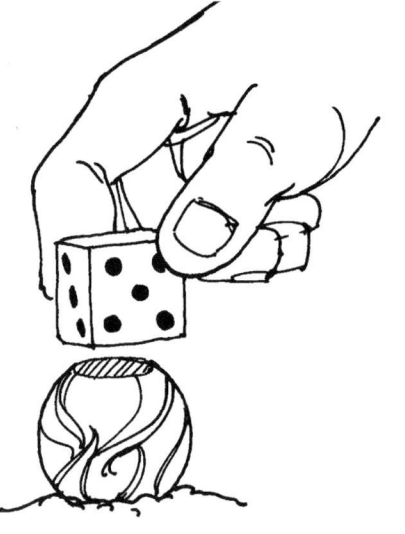

2. One person is the die keeper and draws a taw line five to ten feet from the balanced die.

3. Players take turns shooting at the marble and die, trying to knock the die off its perch. If they fail to do this, the die keeper keeps their shooters.

4. If a player manages to knock the die off, the die keeper must pay that player as many marbles as are shown on the top of the die when it lands.

5. Play continues until everyone has had a shot at the marble, or until the die keeper calls it quits. Another player gets to be die keeper, and the game starts again.

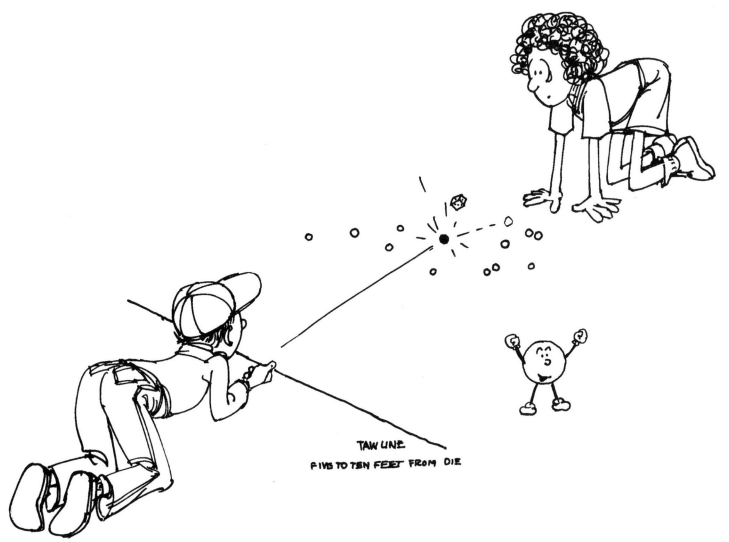

TAW LINE

FIVE TO TEN FEET FROM DIE

Variations:

1. If nobody wants to be the die keeper, players still lose their shooters on a miss, but they must leave the shooters on the ground. Players collect their winnings from the shooters of other players. If there aren't enough marbles on the ground, the player continues to collect lost shooters until all of his winnings have been claimed.

2. Instead of winning and losing marbles, play for points. Set a winning total (make it fairly low, like fifteen or twenty). Players who knock the die off the marble get the number of points shown on the top of the die when it lands. The first player whose scores add up to the total is the winner.

MARBLE BOCCE

A miniature version of the Italian lawn bowling game

Number of mibsters: Two or more
Difficulty: 🔵 🔵
Object of game: To get as close to the mib as possible

1. Mark off a taw line on a smooth stretch of ground. Standing behind the taw line, one player tosses out a large marble (sometimes called a *boulder*) to serve as the mib.

2. Players take turns throwing marbles from behind the taw line at the mib, trying to get as close to it as possible.

3. A player's marble can hit the mib or the other players' marbles without any kind of penalty. In fact, it's a good strategy to try and hit other players' marbles away from the mib.

4. The round continues until every player has bowled five marbles. The player whose marble is closest to the mib gets one point, as well as one point for any other marble he has that is closer to the mib than any other player's marble.

5. All the players pick up their marbles, a different player tosses out the mib, and a new round begins.

6. The first player to reach twenty-one points is the winner.

LAGGING
Much more than just the start of a game

Number of mibsters: Two or more
Difficulty: 🔵 🔵
Object of game: To shoot a marble closest to the tag line without rolling over it

1. Draw two lines about ten feet apart. Standing behind one line, players take turns shooting or throwing a marble toward the other line. Any method of shooting can be used, as long as the player is standing behind the shooting line.

DRAW THE LINES ABOUT TEN FEET APART

2. After every player has had a turn, the winner is determined. The player to get her marble closest to the second line without rolling the marble past the line is the winner. In a game played for keeps, she also collects all the marbles that the other players have shot.

ASSORTED GAMES

A mixed bag of marble games

Is your thumb getting tired yet? Have you run out of places to play the same old shooting games you've been playing for the last few weeks? Here are some nontraditional marble games for you to try out. Some involve good old-fashioned guessing; others will require you to use marbles as substitutes for pieces in new or familiar games. And you thought there weren't any more uses for marbles—read on and find a whole bunch more!

ODDS OR EVENS
Guess right and win a marble

Number of mibsters: Two or more
Difficulty:
Object of game: To guess whether the questioner is holding an odd or even number of marbles

1. One player is chosen to be the questioner.

2. She holds a number of marbles in her hand and asks each player in turn to guess whether she is holding an odd or an even number of marbles.

3. When all players have guessed, the questioner shows how many marbles she is holding. Those who guessed wrong must pay the questioner one marble, and those who guessed right collect a marble from her.

4. The next player becomes the questioner, and the game continues until everyone has had a chance to be the questioner. The player with the most marbles is the winner.

EGGS IN THE BUSH

Bet you can't guess how many marbles you'll win!

Number of mibsters: Two or more
Difficulty: 🌑
Object of game: To guess how many marbles the questioner is holding

1. One player is chosen to be the questioner. He holds a certain number of marbles in his hand, and the other players try to guess how many marbles he is holding. After everyone has guessed, the questioner opens his hand to reveal the right answer.

2. Players who guess correctly are paid the same number of marbles as the questioner is holding.

3. Players who guess wrong pay the questioner the difference between their guess and the number he is holding. For example, if the questioner is holding ten marbles and one player guesses three, that player must pay the questioner seven marbles.

4. The next player becomes the questioner, and the game continues until everyone has had a chance to be the questioner. The player with the most marbles is the winner.

LONG TAW
A chase game for two

Number of mibsters: Two
Difficulty:
Object of game: To chase after the marbles and hit them all

1. Each player contributes one marble to the game. Draw a taw line and place one marble about six feet from it. The second marble should be six feet from the first marble and twelve feet from the taw line, as shown.

2. The first player shoots at the first marble from behind the taw line. If she hits it, she keeps it and shoots again from behind the line at the second marble. If she then hits the second marble, she keeps it too, and the round is over.

SIX FEET FROM TAW LINE TO FIRST MARBLE

3. If she misses the first marble, she leaves her shooter where it ends up. The second player can shoot from behind the taw line at any of the marbles on the ground.

4. The two players take turns shooting at the marbles on the ground, leaving any shooters on the ground when they miss. The round is over when all the marbles have been won.

5. When one round is over, players again contribute one marble apiece, and the game starts again, with the other player shooting first.

Variation:

If one player hits the shooter just used by the other player, she wins all the marbles on the ground.

SIX FEET BETWEEN MARBLES TOO!

GOLF
Make it through the course in the fewest shots

Number of mibsters: Two or more
Difficulty: 🌀 🌐 🌀
Object of game: To complete the course in the fewest shots

This game is played just like the sport, and designing a marble golf course is almost as much fun as playing on it. You'll need a fair amount of room, although you can make the course as big or as small as you like. A smaller course should have plenty of hazards (obstacles) to make it a challenge, but a big course is hard enough without putting extra things in the way.

TAW LINE FOR HOLE FOUR

TAW LINE FOR HOLE FIVE

TAW LINE FOR HOLE THREE

TAWLINE FOR HOLE NUMBER TWO

TEN TO TWENTY FEET

TAW LINE FOR HOLE NUMBER ONE

For hazards, you can use sandpits and puddles (like real golf), dig small holes, or use anything found in your house or yard that will be hard to shoot a marble around. Rocks, sticks, shoes, empty milk cartons, old baseballs, and paperback books are all good hazards, but you're limited only by your imagination.

Real golf courses have eighteen holes, but you can make your course with fewer holes if you want. Each hole should be numbered (pieces of paper with numbers on them can be placed on or near the holes) and should have its own taw line and a shallow hole to aim for. The distance between taw line and hole should be different for each hole—longer for holes without many hazards and shorter for holes that are tough to reach. Try to keep the hole between ten and twenty feet from the taw line. You can increase this distance if you're a good shooter.

1. Marble golf is played just like real golf. Standing behind the taw line for hole one, each player tries to shoot his marble in the hole. Each player takes his first shot in turn, and then play continues with the person farthest from the hole. Everyone should keep track of the number of shots it takes to get his marbles in the hole.

2. Once everyone has gotten a marble into the first hole, everyone starts shooting at hole two from behind its taw line. Continue through all of the holes, making sure that no one starts a new hole before everyone's finished the previous one.

3. The person to complete the course with the fewest shots is the winner.

Variation:
In golf scoring, shots are added for hitting a hazard. If your marble falls in a puddle or knocks into a hazard, add a shot to your score.

MARBLE JACKS

A classic kid's game—now with marbles!

Number of mibsters: Two or more
Difficulty:
Object of game: To pick up six marbles before the ball bounces

Playing with marbles instead of jacks can be more difficult, because marbles are round and slippery and therefore hard to pick up. To play marble jacks, you'll need six marbles and a small rubber ball. If you don't have a small ball, use a marble instead, tossing it in the air instead of bouncing it.

1. Spread out the six marbles on the ground. Players take turns bouncing the ball and trying to pick up the marbles before the ball bounces again.

2. Bounce the ball once and pick up one marble (in the same hand you bounced the ball with) before the ball bounces again. Continue this until all six marbles have been picked up. This is *onesies*.

3. Now spread out the marbles again and repeat step 2, picking up two marbles at a time. This is called *twosies*.

4. Each time a player has picked up all the marbles without a mistake, she continues as in step 2, picking up *threesies* (three marbles), then *foursies*, *fivesies*, and *sixsies*. The first player to complete sixsies wins.

5. If a player makes a mistake at any time, she forfeits the marbles she just picked up and must start again where she made the mistake. Mistakes include: picking up or touching the

wrong number of marbles; allowing the ball to bounce twice before picking up the marbles; or picking up marbles with the wrong hand.

MARBLE MANCALA
An African game updated with marbles

Number of mibsters: Two
Difficulty: 🌀 🌍 🌀
Object of game: To get rid of all the marbles on your side of the board

For this game, you'll need forty-eight marbles, an empty egg carton, and two paper cups. It's best to use the smallest marbles you have and try to find an extra-large egg carton.

1. Divide up the marbles and put four in each bin of the egg carton. Put one paper cup, called a *mancala*, at each end of the carton. The two players sit facing each other across the egg carton.

2. The first player picks up all the marbles in one of the carton bins on his side of the board, and "sows" them. He sows the marbles in his hand, moving clockwise, by putting one marble in each of the other bins and his own mancala. He never places a marble in the other player's mancala.

3. If the last marble is placed in his own mancala, he gets another turn.

4. If the last marble is placed in an empty carton bin on his side of the board, he "captures" the marbles in the bin directly opposite on his opponent's side. He places all these captured marbles, along with the marble he captured them with, in his own mancala.

5. When he finishes his turn, the other player sows all of the

marbles from one of the carton bins on his side. A player can never pick up marbles from a bin on his opponent's side of the board.

6. Players are not allowed to count the marbles in any of their bins. When a player touches the marbles in a bin, he must play them.

7. The game ends when one player has no marbles on his side of the board. The other player adds all the marbles on his side of the board to his mancala. The winner is the player with the most marbles in his mancala.

MARBLE BILLIARDS

You don't need a cue or a table to play this game

Number of mibsters: Two

Difficulty: 🔮 🔮

Object of game: To hit one or more marbles out of the rectangle

1. Mark off a small rectangle (about two feet by four feet) and place fifteen marbles in the center, arranged in a triangle.

2. Players take turns trying to hit one or more marbles out of the rectangle. They can knuckle down from anywhere inside the rectangle to make their shot, and the shooter must end up inside the rectangle for the shot to count.

3. If a player hits a marble out and keeps her shooter inside the rectangle, she shoots again from wherever her shooter ends up.

4. When all the marbles have been hit out, the player who's hit the most marbles out is the winner.

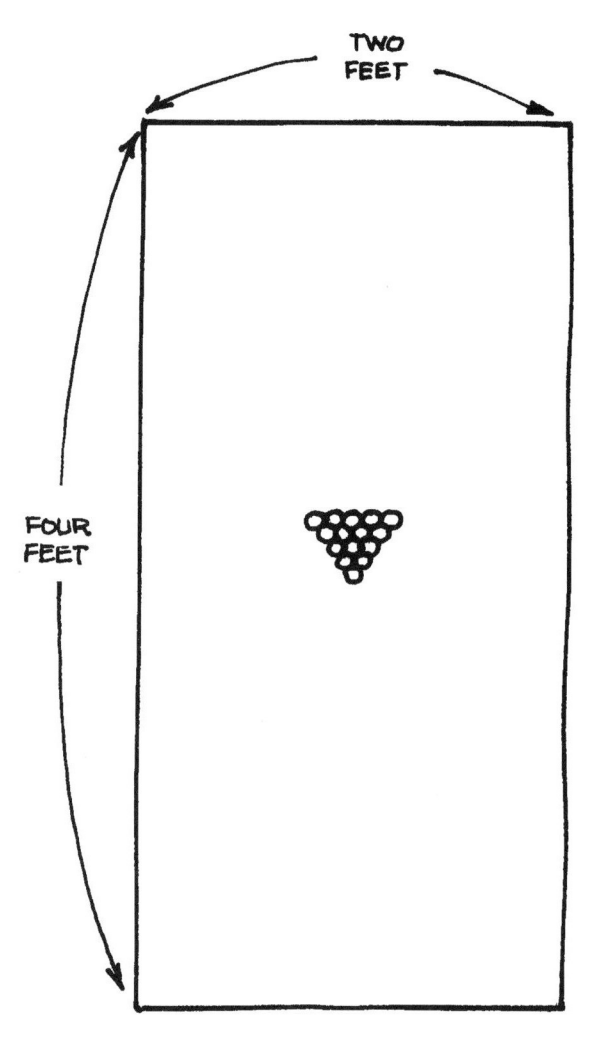

TWO FEET

FOUR FEET

Variations:

1. To play Pool, dig small holes at the corners and one in the middle of each of the long sides (six holes in all). For real pool bank shots, you can plant low walls on the sides, so that marbles can bounce off. Anything flat and hard, such as sturdy cardboard or blocks of wood, will do for walls. Only marbles that land in holes are considered to be hit out.

2. For Eight Ball, you'll need to choose one marble that is different from all the others for the eight ball. It must be the last marble hit out, and if it is hit out before that point, the player who hit it loses. Also, if a player shoots at the eight ball and her shooter leaves the rectangle (whether or not the eight ball does too), she loses the game.

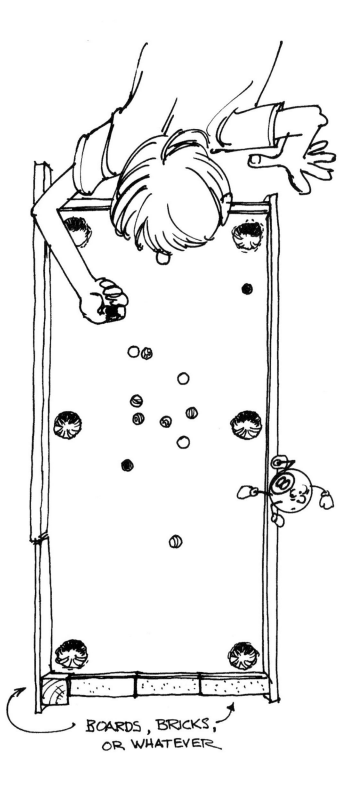

BOARDS, BRICKS, OR WHATEVER

MARBLE CROQUET

Marbles and wickets are all you need for this game

Number of mibsters: Two or more

Difficulty: 🔴 ⚫

Object of game: To be the first to shoot a marble through the course

You'll need nine wickets and two end posts for Marble Croquet. A wicket is a wire arch as wide as two marbles and large enough for a marble to pass under when the wicket ends are pressed into the ground. The end posts can be pens, pencils, sticks, or any small, sturdy rod. A traditional croquet course is set up as shown at right.

1. The first player begins at the first post and shoots through the wickets in the direction indicated by the arrows.

2. Players earn an extra shot for passing through wickets or for hitting the marbles of other players. No more than one extra shot can be earned with a single shot, however. Passing through two wickets, hitting two marbles, or hitting a marble and passing through a wicket with a single shot earns a player only one extra shot.

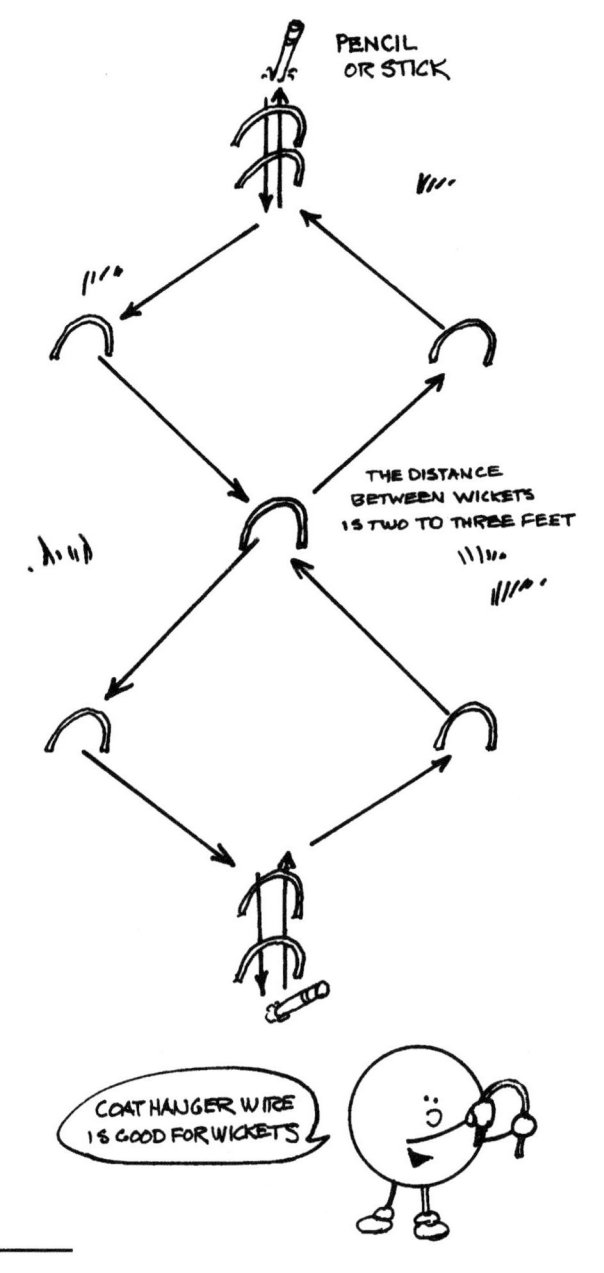

PENCIL OR STICK

THE DISTANCE BETWEEN WICKETS IS TWO TO THREE FEET

COAT HANGER WIRE IS GOOD FOR WICKETS

3. If a player hits another player's marble, he replaces his shooter at the point where it hit the other marble and takes his extra shot from there. The other player's marble remains wherever it stops rolling.

4. When a player reaches the other end post, he must hit the post with his marble before returning through the wickets. Hitting an end post earns a player an extra shot.

5. The first player through the course is the winner.

Variation:
Poison Croquet: When a player finishes the course, he becomes "poison" and can aim for the marbles of other players. Players whose marbles are hit are out of the game, even if those players are themselves "poisoned." The last player in the game is the winner.

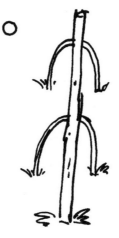

MARBLES, ANYONE?

MARBLE SOLITAIRE
Marble fun just for one

Number of mibsters: One
Difficulty: 🔴 🔴
Object of game: To remove all the marbles but one

1. Begin with thirty-two marbles arranged as shown at right. You can use the carpet, smooth dirt, or even get someone to help you make a board out of wood or clay. Your circle can be any size, depending on how big or small your playing area is. Be sure to leave at least a finger width between marbles so that you can pick up the marbles. The blank space in the middle is the only open hole.

2. The object of the game is to eliminate all the marbles but one. Marbles are eliminated by jumping one over another into an open hole, and the marble jumped over is removed.

3. Jumps can be made vertically or horizontally but not diagonally.

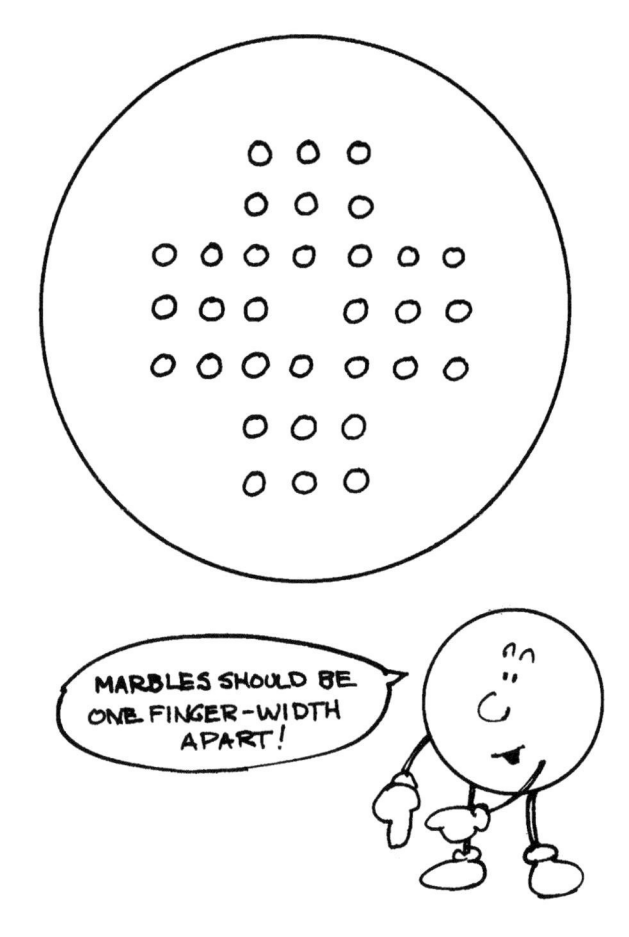

MARBLES SHOULD BE ONE FINGER-WIDTH APART!

4. The game is over when one marble is left, or when no more jumps can be made.

Variations:

1. End up with the last marble in the center hole (the one that began as the only open hole).

2. Move the first open hole away from the center, to any of the other thirty-two positions.

FOX AND GEESE
Don't get trapped by the geese!

Number of mibsters: Two
Difficulty: 🔵🔵
Object of game: To trap the "fox" or get rid of the "geese"

1. Set up a board of thirty-three holes, as shown. It's the same board as in Marble Solitaire, so you can make one or use the carpet or smooth dirt. Arrange seventeen marbles of one color and one marble of another color, as shown.

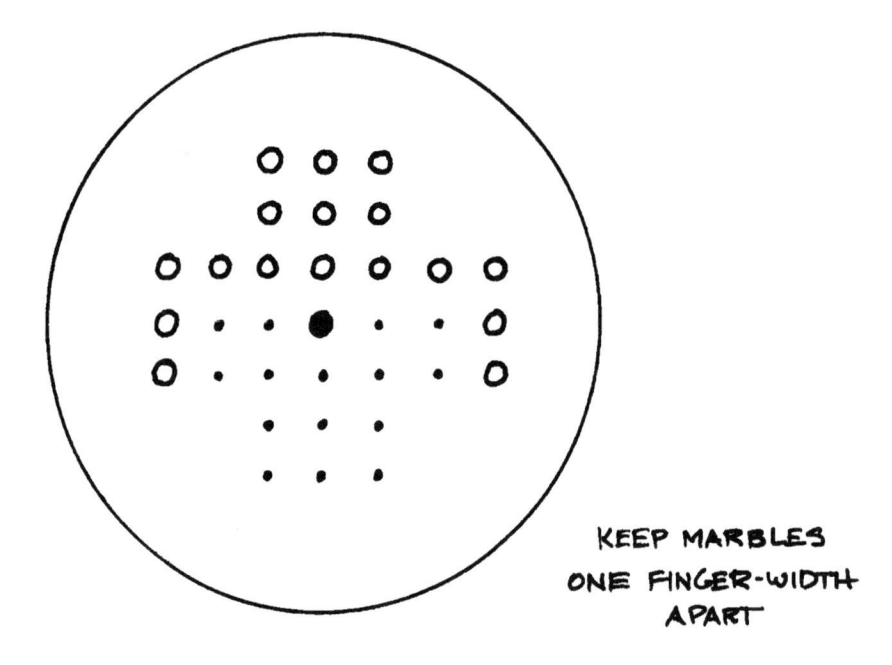

KEEP MARBLES
ONE FINGER-WIDTH
APART

2. The marble in the middle is called the *fox* and is controlled by one player. The other player controls the other marbles, called *geese*. Players take turns moving, one marble at a time.

3. The fox moves in any direction but diagonally, and the geese move forward and sideways, but not backward.

4. In addition, the fox is able to jump over a goose in his turn and remove it. There must be an open hole next to the goose for the fox to be able to jump over it. If the holes are available, the fox can make a series of jumps in one turn (as in checkers) and remove all the geese he jumps over.

5. If the fox is able to jump over a goose but does not, the other player can return one goose to an open spot on his back row.

6. While the fox tries to remove all the geese from the board, the geese try to surround the fox so that he cannot move or jump. When either of these things happens, the game is over.

Variations:

1. Allow the fox to move and jump diagonally too.

2. Change the size and shape of the board to a bigger cross, a circle, or a square.

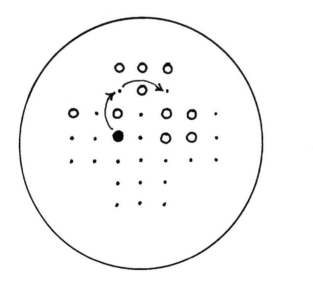

CHINESE TAKE-OUT MARBLES
Eating with chopsticks will never be the same

Number of mibsters: Two or more
Difficulty: ⦾ ⦾ ⦾
Object of game: To move all your marbles from one bowl to the other

1. Each player has two small, shallow bowls and each fills one of his bowls with the same number of marbles (any number is fine, as long as each player uses the same).

OOPS!

2. Using chopsticks, or pencils held like chopsticks, each player tries to move all his marbles from one bowl to the other. Using the eraser end of the pencils makes the marbles easier to pick up.

3. The first player to move all his marbles wins.

OTHER MARBLE ACTIVITIES

A way to use marbles around the house

Marbles can be used in many ways that don't require playing a game. If you ever grow tired of playing with marbles or have won some particularly beautiful marbles that you don't want to risk losing, try some of these suggestions:

- Use them at the bottom of your fish tank or fishbowl. This looks good and gives fish a place to lay eggs.

- Cover the soil of a potted plant with marbles to keep water from evaporating too quickly.

- A jar full of marbles can be placed in a window to catch the light or used to hold up flowers or candles.

- Glue marbles to a sturdy background to make mosaics, sculptures, or other crafts. Glue clearies to glass and make a three-dimensional stained-glass window.

• If you're missing a piece or two from your favorite board game, put a little bit of modeling clay on the bottom of a marble. If the clay isn't too sticky, you should be able to use the marble as a playing piece, then pull off the clay later and still use the marble. If you use a kind of clay that will dry and harden, your marble can become a permanent part of your game.

• Glue a magnet to the back of a favorite marble or group of marbles to make a beautiful refrigerator magnet.

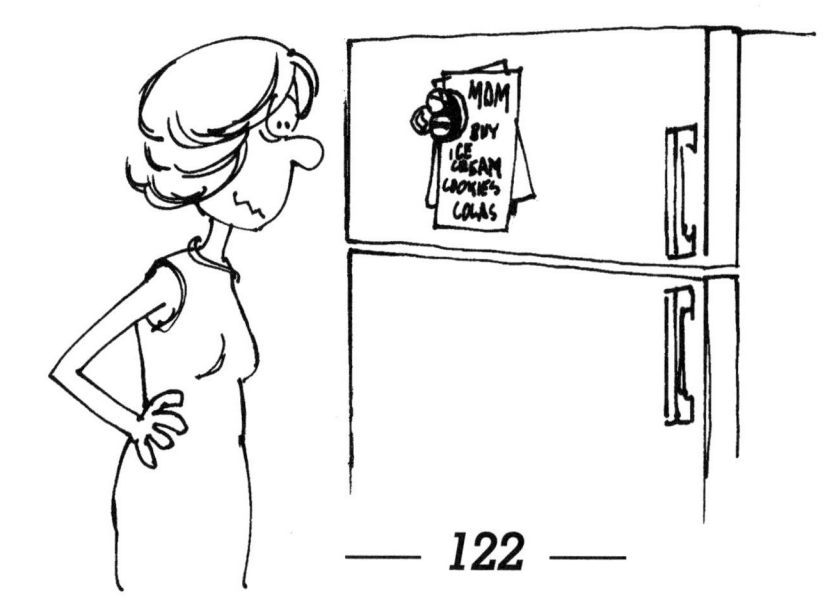

STARTING YOUR OWN MARBLE COLLECTION

Marbles are also fun to collect. The best collections feature a mix of valuable marbles that you can display and more common ones that you can play with—and use to win even more marbles!

Toy and game stores almost always carry mass-produced marbles, which are not very expensive and are good for most keepsies games. If you'd rather display your marbles and play games with them only occasionally, you can try to find rare or expensive marbles. Garage and yard sales are good places to look for bargains on old and valuable marbles. Some antiques stores carry marbles, and you can also visit marble collectors, tournaments, or conventions in your area if you're hunting for a particularly rare marble.

If you want a checklist for your marble collection, take a look at the glossary of marbles on the following pages. There you'll find descriptions of both common and rare marbles. Whether you choose clambroths, cat's eyes, or corkscrews for your collection, the important thing is to make it uniquely your own!

KINDS OF MARBLES

There are many different kinds of marbles, with such exotic names as *lemonade egg yolk,* **peppermint, and** *red banana,* **but here are a few of the basics.**

Aggie   Aggies are marbles made of agate, a mineral that can be brown, reddish brown, gray, yellow, or white. Since agate is harder than glass or clay, some of the best shooters are made from this mineral.

Alley   A marble made of alabaster is called an *alley.* The most valuable kind of alley is a *blood alley,* a white marble streaked with red. Because alabaster—a kind of white marble (rock)—is very expensive, real alabaster marbles aren't made anymore. Nowadays, marbles that only look as though they're made of alabaster are also called alleys.

Bumboozer   (or *boulder, scaboulder,* or *kabola*) Any kind of large marble.

Cat's eye   The single spiral of colors inside this kind of swirl marble (definition follows) looks like the slitted pupil of a cat's eye, which is where it gets its name.

Chinas   Machine-made marbles of clay or porcelain with designs painted on the surface.

Clambroth   A kind of swirl marble that is off-white and opaque with colored stripes on the surface.

Clearie   A marble made of any color of clear glass.

Comic strip marbles   Because they were made for only a short time by a single glassmaker in America, these marbles are very rare. A picture of a comic strip character is printed on the outside of the marble.

Commoney   Some of the first marbles ever made were clay marbles, called *commoneys*. Although many of these were made— their name comes from the word *common*—you'd have to visit an antiques store to find them today. Commoneys are sometimes called *pedabs*.

Corkscrew   A marble with twists of color running from one end to the other.

End-of-day   When a glassblower was done for the day, he sometimes made these marbles from whatever bits of glass were left over. An end-of-day has a mark at one end from the pointil (the glassblower's iron) that shows the marble was made individually and not cut from a rod. An onionskin (definition follows) is a kind of end-of-day marble.

Frosted   These marbles are made by dunking a finished marble in acid.

Gemstones   Very valuable marbles made in Europe from semiprecious stones.

Glassy   A glass marble.

Immie   A glass marble meant to imitate an aggie.

Lustered   (also called *lusters, rainbows, oilies,* and *pearls*) This marble is treated with chemicals to make it look shiny and oily.

Lutz   A swirl marble with sparkling pieces of copper in the stripes.

Mibs   Once this just meant a clay marble, but now any target marble can be called a *mib*. The term *mibster*, meaning marble player, comes from this word.

Mica snowflakes   A clear marble containing flakes of mica, a shiny mineral that reflects light.

Milkie   Any milky white opaque marble.

Onionskin   Antique swirl marbles with so many spirals that their surface is covered with colored stripes. These stripes make the marble look like an onion. Mostly from Europe, these end-of-day marbles were made when glassblowers wrapped layers of colored glass flakes around a clear glass marble.

Peewee   Any tiny marble, usually 1/2" wide or less. These are often made of steel.

Puree   A clearie without any flaws inside it.

Slag   A marble made by melting two different colors of glass together.

Spotted   A clearie or opaque marble rolled in glass chips while still hot in order to melt spots on the surface.

Steelie   A marble made out of steel; usually a ball bearing. These are outlawed at many tournaments because they can chip or crack a glass marble.

Sulphide   These clearies, made in Germany toward the end of the

1800s, have tiny clay figures embedded in the middle and are very valuable.

Swirl   A glass marble with swirls of color, made of fine glass threads, either on the inside or outside of the marble. When the swirl is on the inside, it often surrounds a solid, hollow, or colored core.